This is

THE ROSARY

This is
THE ROSARY

by Francis Beauchesne Thornton

WITH AN INTRODUCTION BY

His Holiness Pope John XXIII

ORIGINAL DRAWINGS BY

Alex Ross

HAWTHORN BOOKS, INC.

Publishers · New York

First Edition, October, 1961

NIHIL OBSTAT

Walter H. Peters, P. H. D.

CENSOR LIBRORUM

IMPRIMATUR

Most Reverend William O. Brady, S. T. D.

ARCHBISHOP OF ST. PAUL

July 29, 1961

To
His Holiness, Pope John XXIII
with filial respect
and affection

Queen of

the Holy Rosary

Queen of the Holy Rosary,
O bless us as we pray
And offer thee our garland
Of roses day by day:
While from our Father's garden,
Where fairest flowers unfold,
We gather to thy honor
Buds red and white and gold.

Queen of the Holy Rosary,
Each mystery blends with thine,
The sacred life of Jesus
In every step divine:
Thy soul was His fair garden,
Thy virgin breast His throne,
Thy thought His faithful mirror
Reflecting Him alone.

INTRODUCTION

On the Rosary

A GLEAM of light is appearing on the horizon for souls who believe in God and believe that His Son Christ Jesus is present in the world to work the salvation and redemption of all men. The holy and pious vision of the blessed Mother of the Savior—*sancta Maria, Mater Dei,* whom the Christian people call upon religiously and confidently in the development of the Rosary—brings together the great and the small to lift up their minds and hearts as one in a way that gains them light and strength and peace.

This prayer—the Holy Rosary—is the simplest and easiest one of all for the Christian people, and Our venerable predecessors have enriched it with much praise and many blessings.

We are not living under any illusions. As has often been true before in the course of history—for *nil sub sole novum*[1]—the period that the world is passing through now is a very serious one: serious and dangerous. At stake are the role in history of whole peoples, the eternal destiny of every man created in the image of God.

We do not usually lift the veil and reveal how the misery in the world and the things that threaten its ruin wring the heart of one who feels it his sacred duty to guard and defend domestic, social and religious order.

But the statistics are there, frightening in their cold presentation of facts that have been supplied to the public by well-informed, competent experts: a general contempt for life, an insane desire for power and domination: a

From a letter from His Holiness, Pope John XXIII, to Clemente Cardinal Micara, dated September 28, 1960, translated from the Italian by the Rev. Austin Vaughan for *The Pope Speaks,* and reprinted as the introduction to this book by special permission of the Secretariat of State of His Holiness.
[1] "Nothing under the sun is new." ECCLES. I, 10—*Ed.*

subtle but stubborn introduction to a false teaching that uses anti-Christian theories and an anti-Christian spirit as the basis for deciding what kind of structure to give to life in society for the masses who are being fed mere counterfeits of the truth.

We have the liveliest interest in the worthy men and the heads of state whom Divine Providence—which plans or permits all things—has placed in high positions over peoples and nations, or who bear very serious responsibilities in national and international assemblies. We follow their work with all Our heart and fervently hope that they will dedicate themselves to safeguarding justice and liberty.

But above all else, in union with the Christian people, we issue an invitation to greater fervor in praying to the Mother of Jesus, and Our Mother, *Maria Auxilium Christianorum, et Regina Mundi.*[2]

How moving the invitation to prayer that St. Bernard suggested for his own times still is today! We mean his words: *"Respice Stellam: voca Mariam."*[3] In hardship, in doubt, when Holy Church or even the whole social order is threatened always think of Mary: *Mariam cogita, Mariam invoca.*[4]

An "Our Father," a "Hail Mary," and a "Glory be to the Father" on our lips; the vision of the mysteries of the life of Jesus and of His Mother before Our eyes; the sigh of a fervent and expectant heart. Oh, what a delight this blessed Rosary is! Oh, what assurance it brings of being heard here on earth and in the eternal heavens!

In reciting the Rosary, the thing that matters is devoutly meditating on each of the mysteries as we move our lips. Therefore, we are sure that Our children and all of their brethren throughout the world will turn it into a school for learning true perfection, as, with a deep spirit of recollection, they contemplate the teachings that shine forth from the life of Christ and of Mary Most Holy.

PP. JOHN XXIII

Sept. 28, 1960

[2] "Mary, help of Christians and Queen of the world."—*Ed.*
[3] "Look at the star; call upon Mary."—*Ed.*
[4] "Think upon Mary, call upon Mary."—*Ed.*

AUTHOR'S NOTE

IN WRITING *This Is The Rosary* I had two purposes in mind. Part One is intended to explain the historical development of the beads and rosary devotion, and the origin and growth of the prayers that make it up. These factual realities are followed by suggestions for some practical means of increasing fervor, devotion and deepening meditation in reciting the rosary, whether in public or in private.

Parts Two, Three and Four of the book are intended to explore the joyful, sorrowful and glorious mysteries, in a hope to make those mysteries more vivid in the mind, imagination and heart.

Part One surveys more than ten centuries of history, and its complex braiding of many-colored strands that eventuated in the rosary we have today. This part of the story I have tried to tell simply and directly, and to avoid personalities and professional disputes, in order that the main ideas of development should stand out clear and unadorned. The story of the rosary is one of ever-increasing Marian devotion, which requires no exaggeration or excessive color in its telling.

After these chief facts about the rosary and its prayers, the mysteries and their fullness of meaning are next considered. Such consideration must dwell first of all on quotations from the New Testament which set the scene for the particular mystery, and which are essential in understanding its meaning and magnificence.

Thirteen of the fifteen mysteries of the rosary are based on quotations from the New Testament.[1] For the last two glorious mysteries, however, the Assumption and the Coronation of Our Lady, we must have recourse to tradition and the apocryphal gospels.[2] For some mysteries, such as the Scourging

---

[1] All New Testament quotations are from *The Holy Bible, St. Peters' Edition, Westminster Text,* Hawthorn Books, New York, unless otherwise specified.

[2] Quotations from the Apocryphal Gospels appearing between pp. 175-188 are not meant to equate these writings with the Holy Scriptures, but to illustrate the vision and piety of the faithful in the early centuries of the Church when these compositions were first current.

and Crowning with Thorns, the Scriptural quotations on which they are based offer us little beyond the barest statement, but the researches of scholars and Scriptural commentators are able to amplify this simplicity with vivid detail. Concerning the great mystery of the Faith, the Resurrection, the Scriptural quotations are abundant of course, but they too require explanation and reordering for their full understanding.

To this essential Scriptural foundation I sought to add imaginative pictures of the action and meaning of each mystery and to incorporate as much as is possible of all that the many learned commentators have written on each particular mystery of the Faith. My purpose here was to make the action of each mystery and its meaning as resplendent and memorable as I could.

All this amounts to an attempt to prepare the self for its encounter with mystery: to touch the very center of human awareness, to sharpen receptivity, to increase, to deepen, to intensify, to exalt.

In one sense, when we immerse ourselves in the mystery of the rosary, we are like pearl-divers plunging into the ocean. The wealth of the precious beauties we may find depends on how well we have armored ourselves for descent into the profound.

In another sense we may be compared with the knowledgeable student who goes to his tutor for instruction: having prepared mind and heart with all available human knowledge, we let the mysteries speak to us of that which is beyond time. So we may gradually learn that simple joys and tragic sorrows must be glorified before they pass from evanescence into immortality. In learning this we come to realize that the mystery of the universe is a divine comedy in which the discords of life are lifted to harmony in the final glorious mysteries. More simply, we learn to look at life whole, and in tranquility.

It is my hope that many people will find in this book all the necessary facts and suggestive sparks to fire their meditation on the mysteries, and to increase their love of our great Mother and her Son.

—FRANCIS BEAUCHESNE THORNTON

Contents

Illustrations

Part One

ORIGINS

AND

DEVOTIONS

I BEADS FOR COUNTING

MAN is by nature inventive. From the wheel to the electronic brain he has pursued a course to make his life easier and less subject to error.

Religious men are no exception to this rule. In those faiths in which a set or complex pattern of prayer is to be followed, some method of counting has usually been found necessary. Each religion solves the problem in its own way, or in the same way, though the same solution may be arrived at for varying reasons.

If it were necessary to count your prayers, what would be the easiest way? Obviously, on your fingers. They are conveniently available wherever you may go, and they provide a decimal pattern that is not too difficult for even the simplest minds, as the actions of children show.

For large sums, however, counting by fingers can be confusing. There is a further disadvantage. In case of interruptions no permanent record remains; one is never completely sure that his total obligations have been met. Something more objective is wanted.

In primitive societies small pebbles served as prayer counters. They can be moved from place to place providing a precise count, or they can be carried in a pocket or sack and can be thrown away as each prayer is completed. But this method too has certain drawbacks. The gathering of stones, the transferring of them from place to place, and the casting away of them, have a tendency to break the thread of concentration. There is also the inconvenience in having to gather the pebbles and the nuisance of carrying them about, especially if the total number of counted prayers is large.

A piece of cord provides a ready solution to some of these problems. It is light enough to be carried through all the activities of the day. The precise number and the exact pattern of prayers can be arranged by a series of knots tied on the cord. In this way, convenience, ease and concentration are all served.

But aesthetic man is still unsatisfied. Cords, however ornamental, soon become soiled and sorry things. Obviously, it is only a step from this conclusion to the stringing of beads on chains, for in this fashion, permanence, cleanliness and convenience may be transfigured into ornament and beauty. And so it was, somewhat in this natural manner of evolution, that beads for counting prayers came into being in all the religions of the world.

The first clear reference to the use of beads for counting prayers is found in the history of Hinduism, but this does not prove that the practice was first invented in Hinduism since any religion with a set numerical pattern of prayer would demand some like method of counting. At any rate, the various Hindustani sects numbered and arranged their prayer beads in conformity with the beliefs and prayer demands of their individual sect.

With the emergence of Buddhism in India, the use of prayer beads spread throughout the Orient. Once again, in shape and arrangement these beads followed the regional practices of Buddhism in Japan, China and Tibet.

It is interesting to note that the practice of repetitious prayer follows and grows with the emergence of meditative religions. In much the same way that a lover repeats stock phrases in praise of his beloved, from the intense need to express the depth of his love, so too mystics of every faith found deepening consolation in voicing over and over their endearments of God.

Even the prayer wheels used in the holiest shrines of Tibet are a spiritual variation on the counting theme. The tiny flags on the wheels each contain the holiest Buddhist prayer, "Hail the jewel in the Lotus." As the light wheel turns, either in the wind or by hand, hundreds of prayers faster than tongue can tell are believed to hail the holy one and deepen the contemplation of his shining beauty.

Islam, with its strong emphasis on short, repeated prayers, had invented its own strings of counting beads within two hundred years after Mohammed. During the two centuries in which the counting beads fought for acceptance, there are references to the more primitive and less exact methods of counting prayers such as fingers and pebbles. As the use of prayer beads spread among the faithful of Islam, the arrangement, raw material and number of beads once again depended on the prayer life of the various sects.

It is a common preconception that the Catholic Church took its prayer beads from the Moslems, who had in turn taken them from the Buddhists. This preconception springs from two sources. Probably the more important of these is the tendency to picture Christianity as a kind of higher paganism, as some armchair philosophers of the nineteenth century did. The second is the fact that the rosary did not come into its widest use until after the Crusades.

It makes a pretty picture to think of some pious Emir seated on his elegant divan fingering his pearl and amber prayer beads between pauses in parley, impressing Christian knights with his magnificence and arousing an urge in them to possess such an ornamental prayer counter. It makes an equally pretty picture to think of Moslem traders first finding their clue to the beads in some turquoise-roofed monastery on the top of the world.

Unfortunately, these are only pretty pictures; it is now certain that bead counters are the natural and inevitable result of the impulse or need to count one's prayers. There is no serious evidence which would prove that either Catholics or Moslems were influenced from without in the evolution of their prayer beads.

In all cases where the independent evolution of prayer beads has taken place, they may ultimately be used in either of two ways. The first is to use them as mere counters and to ascribe to them talismanic importance. The second is to use them as an instrument of release into contemplation, and to value them as such.

It is sometimes customary for Catholic writers to imagine that only the rosary achieves the second use. This is ungenerous, since it is apparent that many holy souls in all religions love God and contemplation. Their prayer beads are as dear to them and as spiritually useful as our own rosary.

II THE EVOLUTION

OF THE ROSARY

THE growth of our rosary into its present shape and form took place over many centuries. The first anchorites in the desert used either their fingers or pebbles for counting the daily number of prayers they set for themselves. Ancient Irish monks followed the same practice, which continues to the present time at the shrines of Ireland as the pilgrims are making their "rounds."

Knotted cords as prayer counters began to appear early in the Middle Ages; some of them, woven with gold or colors, were beautiful. By the fifteenth century, beads as prayer counters were widely used all over the Christian world. They became valuable possessions, since many were made of splendid jewels.

The beads were originally called "pater nosters" because they were first employed to count Our Fathers. In the thirteenth century the use of the beads for counting both Our Fathers and Hail Marys grew in popularity. With the development of devotion to the Blessed Virgin the term *rosarium*, a rose garden, came to be the preferred term for the beads; they were also called *chapelets*, little caps or crowns offered to Mary, or *Corona*, which of course means crown.

The evolution of the rosary as we know it awaited the development of the Hail Mary. This prayer originally was composed of four strophes. The first two embody Gabriel's greeting to Mary:

> *"Hail, full of Grace,*
> *The Lord is with thee."*

The concluding two strophes were from Elizabeth's greeting to Mary.

> *"Blessed art thou among women,*
> *And blessed is the fruit of thy womb."*

The first change came with the addition of the word Jesus, or Jesus Christ.

For hundreds of years this was the standard form of the prayer. Gradually two different variations of the last half of the Hail Mary grew in popularity. The first was "Holy Mary, Mother of God, pray for us," or "Holy Mary, Mother of God, pray for us sinners." The second variation, which probably came from Italy, is the form we use today, "Holy Mary, Mother of God, pray for us sinners, now and at the hour of our death."

In 1568, Pius V, in his revised edition of the *Breviary*, made it mandatory for priests to add the Hail Mary to the Our Father in reciting the Office. From that time on, the complete Hail Mary grew into popular usage all over the world.

The custom of employing 150 Hail Marys is also an evolved one. In the monasteries of the Middle Ages, the prayer life of the monks—ouside the Mass—was based on the 150 psalms of David. The psalms were in Latin, however, and not all the lay brothers and monks were learned. Because of this, it became customary to assign to such monks 150 Our Fathers in place of the 150 psalms. It was more than mere prayer counting, since the monks were required to meditate on each repetition of the prayer with profound attention.

From Ireland and her missionaries came the custom of dividing the 150 psalms into three parts of fifty each and as the rosary grew into a set devotion to Our Lady it followed this division. Each fifty concentrated on one aspect of Christ's life: joyful, sorrowful, and glorious.

At first there was a meditation for each bead. Ordinarily the rhythm of the Hail Mary was broken at the word "Jesus" or "Jesus Christ," and the point of meditation was announced before proceeding with the Holy Mary. Carthusians played a large part in this development.

As a popular devotion, this many-pointed mode of meditation proved to be too complex. An attempt was made to simplify the devotion by providing written cards from which the 150 mysteries could be announced. A more interesting simplification, and an admirable one, was the rosary picture, in which the 150 mysteries could be easily visualized.

In spite of these aids, the 150-mystery rosary proved too clumsy and complex, and around the year 1500 the number of mysteries was reduced to fifteen. The way had finally been cleared for the great popular dialogue prayer which the rosary has become today.

Not all rosaries, even in modern times, follow this pattern, however. The rosary of St. Brigit, or Brigittine rosary, for instance, calls for sixty-three Hail Marys, symbolizing the sixty-three years Our Lady was supposed to have lived on earth. It can scarcely be doubted, however, that the standard rosary is the one most people prefer, though the Brigittine pendant on which the cross hangs has been adopted.

We have now reached the point where we can see in place most of the parts of our rosary. The final evolution came with the addition of the Creed as the first prayer of the rosary, and the doxology at the end of each mystery.

The addition of the Creed as the "hoop" upon which we build the garland of roses composed of *Paters* and *Aves,* came into wide usage about 1500, and soon became the standard practice.

The Gloria began to be used in the sixteenth century, and was gradually adopted everywhere in the seventeenth century. Actually, it is one of the oldest prayers of the Church. The Gloria used in our rosary was prescribed for the use of the whole Church in its sung Office at the Council of Vaison in 529.

When the Dominicans, in their church of Santa Maria Sopra Minerva in Rome, introduced the custom of chanting the rosary in the same fashion employed at Vespers, with the Gloria at the end of each mystery, the practice soon spread to the whole of Europe. The rosary, as we know it, was complete.

In a survey of this kind one can only briefly sketch the many-stranded story through the centuries in which the rosary grew into its present form. The strong influence of the Liturgy is everywhere apparent in the course of that story. From this rich mine the common sense of the faithful, largely under the benign direction of the Dominicans, pre-eminently the order of the rosary, chose those elements which have made the rosary the common office of the people. The developing story is always in the direction of simplification and convenience, except in purpose where the movement is away from simple prayer-counting into the rich depths of contemplation.

III THE SPREAD OF

THE ROSARY DEVOTION

THE evolution of the rosary is a complex story in which various religious orders, noted spiritual directors, and popular love of Jesus and His Mother all played a part.

For the rapid spread of the rosary all over the world we are largely indebted to the Dominicans, and especially to Alanus De Rupe who founded the Confraternity of the Rosary.

From their very beginning the Dominicans showed particular devotion to the Blessed Virgin. It was mainly under Dominican inspiration that small societies were formed all over Europe for the regular recitation of the rosary. However, these scattered efforts awaited an organizing genius to weld them into one massive group with the official support of the Church.

This organizing genius appeared in the person of a great Dominican director of souls, Alanus De Rupe, who in 1470 founded his *Confraternity of the Psalter of Jesus and Mary.*

De Rupe was a tremendous enthusiast. In his writings he was often carried away into fantastic statements and illogical proofs. Zeal, enthusiasm, and his own visionary sense of truth were the touchstones of his existence. He has been harshly dealt with by modern scholars because of his many unprovable assertions, chief of which is the story that the Blessed Virgin gave the rosary to St. Dominic.

Although this story seems to be without historical proof, it is possible to see that it was, in Alan's eyes, no mere invention. St. Dominic's love of Mary, his fiery preaching of Mother and Son in his crusade against the Albigenses, and his influence in the formation of ardent devotion to the Mother of God among his spiritual sons marked him as one of Mary's favorite children.

Furthermore, the astounding success of St. Dominic's works seemed to prove the stamp of Mary's approval on everything he did. To one of Alan's enthusiastic temperament it was a short step to the visionary truth of the Blessed Virgin's gift of the rosary to her favorite son. The approval of Mary was obviously there for all the other works of the Saint. Why should Our Lady's Psalter be left out, especially since Alan himself had such a boundless enthusiasm in spreading the devotion to Mary's Psalter?

Five years after Alan's design for a Rosary Confraternity had been formulated, the same plan, adopted by the Dominican Jacob Sprenger in the Rhineland, received the backing of the Holy Roman Emperor, Frederick III. His interest led in turn to papal approval of the Confraternity under Dominican leadership.

The response was electrifying. People registered in the Confraternity by thousands and hundreds of thousands. Although the leadership of the Confraternity was Dominican, Carthusians, Franciscans and Jesuits cooperated enthusiastically in forwarding and enriching the movement in the century that followed.

The sea-victory of Lepanto on the first Sunday of October, 1571, while the Rosary Confraternities of Rome were holding processions imploring victory, led Pius V to include a commemoration of the rosary in the Mass of that Sunday.

The Dominican Order requested the establishment of a feast of the rosary in 1573. Gregory VII granted the request but he restricted it to those churches in which there was a rosary altar. Clement X extended the feast to all of Spain, and Clement XI finally decreed the observance of the feast for the universal Church in 1716.

The Mass for the feast of the Most Holy Rosary establishes quite clearly that the rosary it celebrates is essentially the Dominican rosary we have today. The *Collect* especially sums up for us the purpose, methods and fruits of the rosary: "O God, whose only begotten Son by His life, death, and resurrection, hath purchased for us the rewards of eternal salvation, grant, we pray, that meditating upon these mysteries in the holy rosary of the Blessed Virgin Mary, we may imitate what they contain and obtain what they promise."

First of all the rosary teaches us, through Mary, to *meditate* on the life, death and resurrection of Our Lord, in which His mother was so intimately concerned. By learning to understand the life of Our Lord through continued meditation on these mysteries, we may hope to form ourselves in their spirit, and by doing so obtain eternal life and the final glory of our own resurrection.

The entire Mass of the rosary feast is a further glorification of the Blessed Virgin, not only for her transcendent purity and beauty, but as the one who can best reveal her Son to us, as she did to Jews and Gentiles long ago in a stable in Bethlehem.

Since 1716, rosary devotion has followed the Church's missionaries all over the world. It has become in many ways the favorite prayer of Catholics, and of many outside the Church as well. The greatest saints have praised and loved the rosary.

Significant among the saints of the rosary is St. Louis Marie de Montfort, known since his canonization in 1947 as "the saint of true devotion to Our Lady." St. Louis lived and worked during the exciting years when the rosary was reaching its final development. He died in 1716, the year in which the feast of the rosary was extended to the universal Church. His life was a flaming crusade in behalf of Our Lady and the rosary was his great weapon, especially against the repellent frigidity of the Jansenists.

In his remarkable book, *The Wonderful Secret of the Most Holy Rosary*, de Montfort described the rosary exactly as it is today in form and arrangement. St. Louis found the rosary to be the mark of Catholics high or low, the key to spiritual depth and progress. De Montfort's treatise is, in fact, the epitome of everything that has been advanced in praise and understanding of Our Lady's chapelet and her role in the economy of the Faith.

From the time of St. Louis to our own times, the rosary has grown in power and influence. Today it reaches into every aspect of Catholic life, and has even ventured into the newest forms of instruction to the masses such as radio and television. One can say, with enlightened hindsight, that the rapid development and growing power of the rosary to touch hearts is not astonishing, however miraculous it may seem.

In the first place, the rosary came into its beginning of universal prominence with the growth of nationalism and multiplication of tongues. Before this time, in the golden period when Latin was the universal language, the Mass was the favorite vehicle for teaching Catholics the mysteries of the Faith. But once the Mass had been locked away in a dead language, it lost a great deal of its teaching power.

Then, in the providence of God, the rosary took over the task of teaching the mysteries of the Faith to the whole world, in much the same way as the Mass had formerly done in its presentation of the seasons of the liturgical year. The rosary, with its similar approach and ease of translation into many languages, has served as a fine teaching vehicle.

It has also, in the estimation of many spiritual writers, prepared and conditioned the minds of Catholics for a more complete and loving understanding of the Liturgy.

IV OUR LADY
APPROVES HER ROSARY

THOUGH the story of Our Lady's gift of the rosary to St. Dominic seems at best a visionary's truth, there can be little doubt that the Blessed Virgin has given complete and formal approval of her rosary.

The success with which St. Dominic pursued his conversion of the Albigenses, through concentration on the mysteries of the Faith, is one of the first dazzling signs given by the Mother of God to those who ask for her assistance. These signs have been multiplied since then a thousandfold in the lives of many saints.

But Mary's approval of her rosary is much more direct and positive than these indirect signs would indicate.

In 1830, when the Mother of God appeared to St. Catherine Labouré, she stressed the necessity of prayer, and emphasized her Immaculate Conception.

At La Salette in the iron reaches of the French Alps, in the year 1846, Our Lady instructed two childish visionaries, Melanie Mathieu and Maximin Giraud, on the constant necessity of prayer. The children asked her what prayers were best for them to say, and Our Lady said the Our Father and the Hail Mary, the two chief prayers of the rosary.

It is significant that at Lourdes Our Lady carried a shining rosary. Still more significant is the fact that she fingered her rosary as Bernadette meditated on the mysteries and said the prayers. Our Lady did so in silence except during the *Gloria,* when she joined Bernadette and spoke out in praise of the Trinity.

This circumstance, which a girl of Bernadette's limited intelligence could hardly have invented, is extraordinary proof of Our Lady's approval of her rosary. Still more is it proof of the truth of what Bernadette saw. It would have been improper for Our Lady to say the Hail Mary, equally nonsensical for her to ask for her daily bread, forgiveness of transgressions, and deliverance from evil. Her spoken praise of the Trinity was in keeping with her conception of herself as the humblest slave of God, regardless of the eminence to which God had promoted her.

Mary's approval of her Psalter at Lourdes became a positive command in the Fátima visions of 1917. The three children were at first directed to say the rosary every day, and to this Our Lady in a later vision added, "Continue to say the rosary every day in honor of Our Lady of the Rosary to obtain the peace of the world. . . ."

Obviously, Our Lady's title of Queen of the Most Holy Rosary was very dear to her. Just how dear it was can be imagined when we recall that the sign given at Fátima on October 13, 1917, was one of apocalyptic splendor: the sun danced in the heavens, and it was seen by thousands gathered in the vast plain around the Cova de Iria. Our Lady had announced herself as the "Lady of the Rosary," and she confirmed her right to this title by a miracle of tremendous power.

It is scant wonder that in the following years the public recitation of the rosary has become something in the nature of a world-wide crusade. Prayer and love are at war with hatred and cruelty, but some faint signs of the ultimate triumph of the Queen of the Rosary shine like first dawn on the distant horizons of the world.

V HOW

THE ROSARY

SHOULD BE SAID

IF MOST people were asked how the rosary should be said, they would probably reply, "With dignity, attention and devotion," which are the directives
given to priests in saying Mass and the Office.

When it is said in public, the rosary is a great dialogue prayer. The chief
purpose behind it is to teach men to meditate on the interwoven lives of Jesus
and His Mother. It is hoped that by deepening their love of Our Lord and
Our Lady, men will come to imitate what they love. By doing so they will
grow in goodness and holiness.

Yet it must be admitted that both public and private recitation of the
rosary is often marred with haste and carelessness, as if priests and people
grudged the short time taken up by this devotion. It can hardly be maintained that dignity, attention and devotion are served by rapid, slovenly and
empty-sounding prayer. Men of genuine piety are repelled by such carelessness; those outside the Church often come to visualize the rosary as a kind of
celestial numbers racket.

Certainly there is no attempt here to judge anyone. No one but God reads
the heart aright. But the worship of God does deserve the best, and that implies dignity and beauty. Without these, God's worship appears superficial
and insincere.

This is not to say that people should recite the rosary as if it were some
kind of play-acting. Dramatic overemphasis can be just as annoying as haste
and carelessness, but there is a golden mean, between the two extremes, which
I can best emphasize by telling a story.

When I was in residence at Oxford, in the early thirties, it was my privilege to know Dom Bede Jarrett, the great Dominican writer, preacher and spiritual director. Dom Bede was a most unusual man. Tall and distinguished-looking, with a fine sense of humor, his casually direct manner of speech was immediately impressive.

Growth in his friendship revealed an amazing balance in all his thoughts and actions and a kind of joyousness in everything he did. A certain sweetness came out of the man, as if he were in possession of some radiant secret unknown to others.

What the secret was I came to recognize by listening to Father Bede saying his prayers. It was a memorable experience to hear the rising and falling cadences of Father Bede's light voice, so attentive to every inflection of the language and every nuance of meaning in the community prayers in Latin. In saying the rosary he revealed the same admirable qualities.

Summing it up, I said to myself, "He speaks every prayer as if he meant it with all his heart." Those who can do that, I recognized at once, are holy men in the fullest meaning ot the term, and the joyful secret of Bede's personality was sanctity.

After his untimely death in 1934, at 53, what my intuition had told me from hearing him pray was amply borne out. Many of those who had known him best came forward to testify that they considered Father Jarrett a saint, and the first steps have already been taken to forward the cause of his canonization. There was nothing pompous or obtrusive in Dom Bede's piety. So unusual was his humor and joy of life that I would never have suspected his holiness if I hadn't heard him pray aloud.

To say each prayer as if you meant it—that is the correct way of saying the rosary. Sincerity should ring through the lovely phrases of the rosary prayers, as an indication of the loving and attentive heart from which they come.

In this fashion we can arrive at the proper sense of pace in saying the rosary: neither too fast nor too slow; neither slurred nor dramatically overemphasized; always with sincere appreciation of its meaning.

There may be some who think that concentration on the prayers of the rosary and on the correct manner of saying them is an impediment to meditation on the mysteries, which is of course, the chief end in saying the rosary. But certainly this is not true of the Creed, the Our Father and the Gloria, which stand by themselves and could not possibly interfere with meditation.

As for the Hail Mary, far from impeding meditation, this great prayer should forward and deepen meditation on the mysteries.

All the mysteries have their beginning in the Incarnation, which the Hail Mary sums up over and over for us, as we move along through the joyous, sorrowful and glorious cycles of the rosary. She who was "full of Grace" and "blessed among women," she who intercedes for us with her Son, can also inspire us to see the beauty and splendor of the events that follow the Incarnation.

The steady flow of these oft-repeated and well-remembered words, like the hum of a powerful dynamo, is able to soothe and guide us in concentrating on the joys, sorrows and glories of the great Mother and her Son.

VI THE PRAYERS

OF THE ROSARY

1 The Apostles' Creed

THE Creed we say on the cross of the rosary is known as the Apostles' Creed.

According to one fairly old tradition, the Apostles' Creed was formulated on Pentecost. Each of the Apostles contributed one section and from that time forward it was handed down by word of mouth to all those who entered the Christian community through the rite of Baptism. However, this legend of the making of the Creed has been very largely exploded by responsible Catholic scholars. Today few, if any, would try to maintain or prove the story.

According to a second tradition, St. Peter and St. Paul were the originators of the Apostles' Creed. In times of persecution or heresy, this story has it, the profession of this creed was a symbol of orthodoxy and a convenient way for Christians to recognize one another. Because of the dangerous times it was handed down orally among Christians, but eventually, first in the Liturgy, and later in an ancient Roman Creed, the written Creed emerged.

There is considerable evidence that the Creed, although not exactly as we have it, does go back to apostolic times. When the apostles and disciples were making converts from the pagan world in vast numbers they would almost be forced to formulate some short declaration of basic beliefs. Our Lord was a great teacher, and the things He taught had to be believed if one expected to join His kingdom and attain eternal life.

In any event, the Creed as we have it today is the lineal descendant of the old Roman Creed, a profession of ancient and basic truths taught since the beginning of Christianity.

The Creed is a series of eight pictures. The first portrays the majestic power of God the Father in His creation of the universe. In order to appreciate that picture we ought to turn to the book of Genesis and read the complete story there.

The second picture in the Creed covers the principal events of the New Testament. It shows us who Christ is, and tells the story of His life, death and resurrection, His ascension into the rule of the universe, and His last coming to judge us.

The third picture prefaced once again by a solemn "I believe," brings us to the Holy Ghost. Two things are here worthy of note. The first three sections of the Creed refer to the three persons of the Blessed Trinity. They come first because Christianity is based on belief in the Trinity. The story of Our Lord takes up the largest section since "no one comes to the Father" except through His Son, Whose death redeemed us and prepared the way for the sanctifying work of the Holy Spirit.

Christ's life is the way we must follow, and the Creed holds it high for us to see in all its beauty.

Next in importance is the Church: through her, men come to participation in the "communion of saints, the forgiveness of sins, the resurrection of the body, the life everlasting" with the Blessed Trinity.

The Creed, then, embodies the faith of apostolic days such as we find it set down in the ancient Roman Creed, with a word or phrase added in time for the sake of making its meaning more precise. It takes us back through time to the company of the apostles, when faith blazed out so triumphantly that the whole Roman world was converted to Christianity within 300 years. Standing so near in time to Our Lord in this apostolic profession, we too may hope to catch something of the apostles' fire and zeal in spreading that faith through the world: not the mere zeal of the activist, but actual, personal holiness, which we may hope to increase through loving contemplation of the mysteries of the Rosary.

The Creed is indeed the hoop on which we string the crown of flowers offered to God's Mother. It is through firm belief that we can enter into the climate of the holy mysteries and begin to live with God.

2 The Our Father

After Our Lord's fast in the desert for 40 days and nights, He was tempted by the devil and put the tempter to flight. Then, hearing that St. John the Baptist had been arrested, Jesus came into Galilee and dwelt in Capharnaum, by the Sea of Galilee. There He selected His first disciples among the fishermen: Peter and Andrew his brother, and the sons of Zebedee, James and John.

Jesus began His work at once, preaching the gospel of His kingdom. People began to throng about Him, because of His astounding miracles of healing, and this was the moment He chose to enunciate in the Sermon on the Mount the fundamental rules of His kingdom.

The scene is memorable. There are massive crowds on the sea strand, backed by the blue glitter of sun-shot water. Seated on the green hillside above the crowd, Jesus joyfully announces His gospel of love, beginning with the eight Beatitudes. And it was in this sermon, as St. Matthew presents it, that Jesus gave us His ideal prayer, the Our Father.

He prefaced the prayer with a pointed introduction and followed it with a grand summation, which we need to recall often if our prayers are to follow the direction Jesus gave us:

"And when ye pray, ye shall not be like the hypocrites; for they love to stand at prayer in the synagogues and at the street-corners, in order that they may be seen by men. Amen I say to you, they have already their reward. But thou, when thou prayest, 'enter thy chamber and shut thy door and pray' to thy Father who is in secret; and thy Father who seeth in secret will requite thee. And in your prayers *babble not, as do the gentiles;* for they think to be heard *by reason of their wordiness.* Be not therefore like to them; for your heavenly Father knoweth what things ye need before ye ask Him. Pray ye, therefore, thus:

> *"Our Father in the Heavens,*
> *Hallowed by Thy name,*
> *Thy kingdom come,*
> *Thy will be done,*
>   *as in heaven, so on earth!*

Give us this day our daily bread,
And forgive us our debts,
    as ourselves have forgiven our debtors,
And lead us not into temptation
    but deliver us from evil.

"For if ye forgive men their transgressions, your heavenly Father will likewise forgive you; but if ye forgive men not their transgressions, neither will your Father forgive you your transgressions." MATTHEW VI, 5–15.

Thus we are told that our prayers must be sincere. We are warned not to let our prayers become mere wordiness and babble, in which the lips speak but not the heart. We are also instructed to *ask* the Father, Who knows what we need, but wishes us to ask for it. We are reminded that we cannot hope to be heard unless we first forgive all those who have offended us, for forgiveness is the key to God's bounty. The hating heart is a closed heart, and neither grace nor light can enter it.

An analysis of the Our Father is an analysis of the correct method of prayer. Like children around the table of life we look up to our Father in heaven and wish all men to recognize and revere His holy name. We ask that His kingdom of the spirit be spread throughout the world and that His will (love) shine out over the world as it does in heaven. We are directed to love God and our fellow men whatever befalls us, whatever life may bring us of suffering, sorrow or injustice.

In the second half of the Our Father, we ask God for the necessities of life from day to day, like the birds of the air and the lilies of the field. We ask His forgiveness of our sins by opening the way to forgiveness through our forgiveness of those who have hurt or injured us. We also implore God to permit us not to go into the ways of temptation: the occasions, places, persons and things so often important in leading us to sin.

The last petition, "deliver us from evil," is a great cry to God asking His assistance in keeping us uncorrupted from all the moral evil of the world.

In the Creed we enter the *climate* of faith for the recitation of the rosary. We profess our firm trust in the truths God has revealed to us. In the Our Father we progress to the *mood* of the rosary. Love of God and forgiveness of all must be in our hearts if we are to receive God's gifts and penetrate into the full meaning of the mysteries on which we are meditating.

By means of the prayer Jesus taught us we can hope to achieve that quiet and tranquility of heart in which the Spirit of God may inspire us with wisdom and understanding.

3 *The Hail Mary*

An angel speaks to us in the opening phrases of the Hail Mary, "Hail, full of grace, the Lord is with thee."

The angel speaking those words is Gabriel, one of the great archangels privileged to stand in the sight of God all day. And Gabriel's message is not merely his truth; it is God's truth. Mary is "full of grace," like a precious goblet so filled with wine that not one drop may be added. She is perfect in every way by God's gracious gifts to her in His overshadowing love.

To these opening phrases of the Hail Mary, Elizabeth, directly inspired by God, adds God's further praise of Mary, "Blessed art thou among women, and blessed is the fruit of they womb."

The words we say in the first half of the Hail Mary are holy words since they are God's. They embody the highest praise ever given by God to a human being. Examining carefully all the great personalities of the Old Testament, we find in every one of them some tragic flaw or imperfection. Abraham, Jacob, David, Solomon and all the others, though granted many favors by God, did not perfectly correspond with His love. Now, through the loving mercy of God, a new age had dawned for the world, the perfection of humanity was given to a woman, and her correspondence with that love was perfect in every way.

Contemplating the mystery of the Incarnation and God's praise of Mary, the piety of men added the last half of the Hail Mary: "Holy Mary, Mother of God!" She who was full of grace and blessed among women is given her greatest title, Mother of God.

From her divine maternity other great truths flow: such as her Immaculate Conception, her Assumption, her role as Co-Redemptrix of the human race. Having been given to us on the cross as our Mother, we can hope that she will intercede for us sinners, because she is the link between us and God.

That the Hail Mary has become one of the most loved prayers among Catholics is not surprising. The mysteries of God and His judgments are high and holy, difficult to understand; there is a tinge of fear in them. But with Our Lady it is different. Most of us love our mothers, and through the warmth of such human love we come to value and understand the love of our heavenly Mother. We look to her in all the affairs of life. We ask her mother's heart for a share in the tenderness she gave to Jesus—every day and in the bitter hour of His death.

4 The Gloria

The Gloria is a gravely beautiful prayer to the Blessed Trinity. Formulated in the early years of Christianity, the Gloria reached up to praise the topmost mystery of our religion. Before the sun and the dew and the rain, before light, before the stars were created, before the galaxies fled across the heavens, the mystery of God three-in-one *is*. Looking back until the brain reels, the brightness and the love are there; looking forward beyond the centuries, beyond time and light years, their splendor will be undimmed, will be younger still than the youngest morning of returning spring.

The Trinity is the mystery of mysteries, and because of this it is fitting and beautiful that it should close each of the fifteen mysteries of the rosary. Each event of joy, sorrow or glory, goes back to the Triune God: the Father Who made us, the Son Who redeemed us, and the Holy Spirit Who sanctifies us and dwells within us. Theirs is the glory; Theirs is the achievement of all things beautiful in heaven and earth.

And the Mother of God is the rainbow arching between heaven and earth; the bridge over which God came to dwell among us as man, and Who made us sons by adoption, that we too might own such a Mother to love and intercede for us.

In this moment of revelation, all through the rosary, we can savor for a little the blinding splendor that bends down to us with eternal life.

VII THE MEANING

OF MYSTERY

OFTEN when people speak of the mysteries of the rosary they do so with considerable confusion. The term mystery, for most of us, is a fuzzy one. If called upon to explain the word to children, or to those outside the Faith, many Catholics would do so with stammering confusion.

A look into a dictionary will scarcely lessen this confusion. The unabridged dictionary sets down eight meanings of mystery, which is derived originally from the Greek word *mysterion*. Before the first definition of mystery is a preamble which says, "secret worship of a deity, secret thing." This is followed by the first of the eight meanings, "Something unexplained, unknown or kept secret."

Moving down to the seventh meaning, we find the following: "in *Christianity,* a) the Mass; b) a sacrament, especially the Eucharist; c) any of fifteen events in the lives of Jesus and Mary serving as a subject for meditation during the saying of the rosary."

This is followed by the eighth meaning: "in *theology,* any assumed truth that cannot be comprehended by the human mind but must be accepted on faith."

Here is a plenitude of meanings, but they are of little help in understanding what we mean when we refer to the mysteries of the rosary. If we use that part of the seventh definition which applies specifically to the rosary, "any of fifteen events in the lives of Jesus and Mary serving as a subject for meditation during the saying of the rosary," we have a mere description of the fact, but no real enlightenment.

The Catechism of our early childhood defined a mystery as "something we cannot fully understand." This is a neat summary, but here again it asks almost as much as it answers, when used as an explanation of the mysteries of the rosary.

The confusion we discover in our own minds, and in the dictionary, I think, springs from the fact that the *mysterion* of paganism, referring to Eleusis and other holy places, has one meaning, while the use of the word in the Christian liturgy and theology has quite another.

What is needed is a return to the word's original meaning and usage, back in the times when it was first used in Christian liturgy. There we discover the key to our problem in finding that a mystery in the Christian sense is said to be "something of which part of the meaning can be known on earth, and part of the meaning in eternity."

Applying this to the rosary mysteries, we can see at once how beautifully and accurately it fits. In the Annunciation, for example, we can understand how an angel might appear to a humble virgin of Nazareth. But how the power of the most high should overshadow Mary, in the birth of God's Son, involves an understanding of God and His mercy before which the mind halts. So it is with the other mysteries: part or parts of them have a meaning here for us, part or parts of them will be understood in eternity.

This gives us some clues that will prove useful later on in meditating on the mysteries of the rosary. What can be known by us here should be investigated and explored. Then perhaps, as we meditate, the Holy Spirit will give us the grace to penetrate into the brightness of the eternal part of the mystery.

VIII AIDS FOR

THE MIND

AND THE IMAGINATION

WE HAVE already said something about the pace at which the rosary should be said, and the attention, dignity and devotion that should be characteristic of its recitation. But saying each prayer of the rosary as if you meant it from the heart does far more than govern the pace at which the rosary is said. It slows the tempo of the recitation so that the mind is given more scope for meditation. It also gives meditation deeper meaning, for without understanding the sense of the prayers, meditation becomes a confused exercise.

When you recite the Creed with loving attention you place yourself in the climate of faith.

When you proceed to the announcement of the first mystery you place your mind and imagination within a given set of circumstances, part of them significant here, part in eternity.

In the Visitation, for instance, your mind is entering a known scene, occupied by certain people. It helps both mind and imagination to learn as much about the setting as possible.

Elizabeth's house was, very probably, much like Eastern homes today: white-walled and flat-roofed and built about a patio or a garden. It is good to see the sun, shafting light from leaves and flowers there, while Elizabeth, heavy with child, goes about the usual household tasks, all unsuspecting that Mary is coming to see her.

In this mystery there are only two visible characters, Mary and Elizabeth, but in the dramatic confrontation of the two persons we sense the power of the unseen God hovering over the house, inspiring Elizabeth to cry out in praise of her cousin.

To picture in this way the scenes and persons of each mystery is one of the greatest aids to deepening meditation on the rosary. And in achieving this end, the first practical step is to read what the New Testament says. For all but the two final glorious mysteries, the inspired words of the Scriptures are our best foundation stones.

Next in importance to the Bible are the many well-written and accurate lives of Our Lord and the Blessed Virgin. Scholarly research has thoroughly sifted everything known of the Holy Family and the historical period in which they lived on earth. Such material, in the hands of a talented writer, becomes a vivid re-creation of Jesus and His age, in which we can see Our Lord moving through the lights and shadows of time. As we know, love waits on knowledge.

To the riches contained in Scripture and the lives of Christ, great art and great poetry can add still more. Art, in particular, helps us to visualize the drama in all its splendor of setting, persons, color and form. Often, too, as in El Greco's superb *Descent of the Holy Ghost,* something of the mystical and eternal significance of the scene, certainly some of its emotional meaning, flashes forth to enthrall us.

It would be of tremendous help to most people if parish Rosary Societies were to collect good reproductions of great artists' pictures of the fifteen mysteries. They could be placed on display in the parish hall or school during the months of May and October, or even every week after Fátima devotions.

Remember, however, that I am speaking of great art and great artists. Sentimental, saccharine and insipid works of art should all be ruled out. Great scenes demand great interpretation, and a high altitude of approach to them. Only masterly art provides this.

We do not know exactly what Our Lady looked like. That she was beautiful we may well believe, for both in mind and body she was full of grace, and fair as the "lily of the lilies of the valley."

It is significant, in this connection, that great artists have presented the Blessed Virgin in many ways: sometimes as blonde with blue eyes; sometimes with dark eyes and raven hair. These and the variations and shades between them have helped us to see Our Lady as all things to all men: in the Orient she is pictured as an Oriental; to the African mind, she is black. What one loves most is ascribed to her, because she is the Mother of Men, and takes to her heart all the sorrows and sadness of the world.

Our Lord, being both man and God, is the hardest to capture in art, yet fine art has attempted the task in many dazzling ways that help us to picture Him with vividness and distinctness.

Good poetry, too, can assist us materially in our meditations on the rosary. Poetry today may have less appeal than art, but the few who love it will find it a strong staff for inspiring meditation.

In actually saying the rosary I find it helps me to linger with attention on each phrase of the Creed, Our Father and Gloria. Occasionally I pause in saying the Hail Mary, in order to realize its full meaning, and then return to the meditation on the particular mystery with the thought that the ascending curve of the mysteries is based on the Annunciation and the part Our Lady plays in showing us the beauty of Jesus.

What cannot be overemphasized is the fact that we need to consider far more than the facts of the rosary. In its conception, organization and prayers, it is poetry, and it is for the poetry of the rosary that the mind hungers. Joy, sorrow and glory are caught for us in the fifteen mysteries in much the same splendor in which, for example, the great mosaic in San Appolinaris, outside Ravenna, catches the mystery of the Transfiguration in gorgeous and poetic symbolism.

The more we feed our imaginations the easier it will be to meditate with profit on the mysteries of the rosary. The more often we meditate properly, the deeper we shall penetrate into the divine life, and the more we shall make it a pattern for our own.

Part Two

THE

JOYFUL

MYSTERIES

IX INTRODUCTION TO
THE JOYFUL MYSTERIES

THE joyful mysteries of the rosary are mostly based on the Gospel of St. Luke. This Gospel, which has been called the "most beautiful book in the world," is noted for its quality of supreme joy. For St. Luke, the Gospel is more than good tidings. It is *glad* tidings that can cheer and illuminate all those who sit in darkness and the shadow of death.

In his prologue, addressed to the convert Theophilus, St. Luke tells us that he is writing an "orderly" account of the life of Our Lord based on the testimony of eyewitnesses, who saw the events at first hand. In making this statement Luke does not rule out the possibility that he consulted all the existing documents and written records in addition to oral testimony.

Tradition has it that St. Luke obtained his facts about the childhood of Christ from Our Lady. The intimate sureness with which he deals with this first part of his Gospel, which is not found elsewhere, would seem to indicate that Luke's source was reliable enough to be beyond question by all those persons still living who had been intimately associated with Our Lord and His Mother.

St. Luke, as we know, was a doctor. That his medical knowledge and personality were of unusual caliber is evident from the fact that he was called the "beloved doctor." Then, too, the pure Greek beauty of St. Luke's writing style can be brought forward as further proof of his rich personality.

As a science, medicine demands intense concentration and specialization; its source books are obviously factual, not literary. Thus it is only the most extraordinary physicians who have the ability or inclination to cultivate beauty of style. If we add to this St. Luke's ability to invest his glad tidings with compelling drama, we realize at once that we are reading the words of a most unusual man.

Tradition adds one fact more to those already noted. It has been persistently maintained that St. Luke was an artist. There are in existence several ancient Byzantine portraits of Our Lady which have been ascribed to St. Luke, and several statues as well. Also attributed to him is the portrait of Our Lord which has long been venerated in the ancient papal chapel at the top of the Holy Stairs in Rome. When we contemplate St. Luke's unusual facility in drawing wonderful word pictures, which have been used by most of the great artists of the world, it is easy enough to imagine that he may have been equally skilled with brush or chisel.

At any rate, like a good artist of his time, St. Luke followed Aristotle's advice that literary works should have a beginning, a middle and an end and started his Gospel at the *beginning* of the dramatic events which tell the story of our salvation.

The Old Testament stated in many places that the Messias would have a *precursor*—someone who would prepare the way for His apostolate and revelation. That there was confusion concerning the prophecies is evident in the episode narrated in the first chapter of St. John's Gospel.

The Jewish authorities were disturbed by the Baptist's fiery preaching. So "they sent from Jerusalem priests and Levites to ask him, 'Who art thou?'

"He confessed and did not deny; and he confessed, 'I am not the Christ.'

"And they asked him, 'What art thou then—Elias?'

"And he said, 'I am not.'

" 'Art thou the Prophet?'

"He answered, 'No.'

"They said therefore to him, 'Who art thou, that we may give an answer to them that have sent us? What sayest thou of thyself?'

"He said, 'I am "the voice of one crying in the wilderness, Make straight the way of the Lord," as said the prophet Isaias.'

"And there had been sent some of the Pharisees; and they asked him and said to him, 'Why then dost thou baptize, if thou art not the Christ, nor Elias, nor the Prophet?'

"John answered them, saying, 'I baptize with water; in the midst of you standeth one whom ye know not, even he who cometh after me, the strap of whose shoe I am not worthy to loose.' " JOHN I, 19-27.

St. Luke cuts through this uncertainty by showing us the precise position of the Baptist and the role he will play in preparing the way for Christ and

His kingdom. St. Luke establishes clearly that John the Baptist *was* the *precursor* and that he came to prepare the way for Christ and not to found any party or sect of his own.

St. Luke gives us the *who* and *why* of St. John the Baptist. But he does far more in revealing in dramatic fashion the links between St. John and Christ, such as their relationship and the angelic revelation shared by Mary and her cousin Elizabeth. Furthermore, in narrating the story of the Baptist's promise St. Luke establishes the high pitch at which he will tell his glad tidings, an eminence of the unusual and miraculous, yet superbly natural because of the classical restraint with which the story is told.

St. Luke opens his story by taking us to the holiest spot in Jerusalem— the temple of God. But the temple is more than holy; it is the center of Jewish worship, linked to the glorious past and all that is greatest and most admirable in Jewish history. It also looks forward to the kingdom of God on earth, with the coming of the long-promised Messias.

"In the days of Herod, King of Judaea, there was a certain priest named Zachary, of the course of Abijah; and he had a wife who came of the daughters of Aaron, and whose name was Elizabeth. Both were just before God, walking without blame in all the commandments and ordinances of the Lord. And they had no child, for Elizabeth was barren; and they were both advanced in age.

"Now when he was exercising his priestly office in the turn of his course before God, it came to pass that he was chosen by lot, as was the practice of the priestly service, to enter the sanctuary of the Lord and to burn the incense. And the whole multitude of the people were without at the hour of the incensation. And there appeared to him an angel of the Lord, standing at the right of the altar of incense. And Zachary was troubled at the sight, and fear fell upon him. But the angel said unto him, 'Fear not, Zachary, for thy petition hath been heard. And thy wife Elizabeth shall bear thee a son, and thou shalt call his name John. And thou shalt have joy and gladness, and many shall rejoice in his coming, for he shall be great before the Lord. And "he shall take no wine or strong drink," and shall be filled with the Holy Spirit even from his mother's womb; and many of the children of Israel shall he turn to the Lord their God. And himself shall go before him in the spirit and power of Elias, "to turn the hearts of fathers to their children" and the disobedient to the wisdom of the just, to prepare for the Lord a ready people.'

"And Zachary said unto the angel, 'Whereby shall I know this? For myself am an old man and my wife is advanced in age.'

"And the angel answered and said to him, 'I am Gabriel who stand before God; and I have been sent to speak unto thee and to bring thee these glad tidings. And behold, thou shalt be dumb and unable to speak until what day these things have come to pass, because thou hast not believed my words, which shall be fulfilled in their time.'

"And the people was waiting for Zachary and wondering that he tarried in the sanctuary. But when he came forth he was unable to speak to them; and they realized that he had seen a vision in the sanctuary. And he kept making signs to them and remained dumb.

"And it came to pass that when the days of his service were completed, he departed to his home.

"Now after these days Elizabeth his wife conceived; and for five months she hid herself away, saying, 'Thus hath the Lord dealt with me in the days wherein he hath seen to the removal of my reproach among men.'" LUKE I, 5-25.

THE FIRST

JOYFUL MYSTERY

The Annunciation

HAVING created this luminous atmosphere, St. Luke proceeds with the main plot of the story which has become the first mystery of the Rosary.

Six months after the angel had appeared to Zachary in the temple, God sent Gabriel on his second and most important mission. Accordingly, the spotlight shifts from the center and head of the Jewish religion to Nazareth, a little-known town of Galilee, ruled by the odious King Herod.

Nazareth was a country town on the northern border of the great plain of Israel, a cluster of limestone houses huddled like sheep at the edge of the hills, covered with groves of pine and cypress. Tradition tells us it was spring, and we can imagine how beautiful spring could be in those far-off days when the land was unplagued by drought and still, as the Biblical phrase describes it, "flowing with milk and honey."

The grass in the fields and meadows would be sun-green. Black-green hedgerows framed the green squares of wheat, dotted with anemones. These were the lilies of the field Our Lord spoke of, clothed more beautifully than King Solomon in all his glory. The promise of spring in Nazareth would be apparent in the silver olive trees and in the new shoots on the vines, that felt for the light and promised grapes for new wine. A green shout of gladness rang to the far edge of the sky. Motes of golden sun danced in the shafts of light.

Against this rich background of star and sky and flower, the outwardly-simple but inwardly-rich lives of the people were lived out. They rose with the sun and worked at the old tasks man has known since he settled down from his nomadic wanderings to cultivate with loving care the fruitful places of the earth. There was planting, hoeing and weeding to be done by the men. Spinning, weaving and dyeing, in addition to the household tasks, were the work of the women.

Nazareth was unknown to most of the world outside Palestine. But God was watching Nazareth, where Mary lived, with the same fidelity as the great eye of the sun blazing down on the white-walled houses.

St. Luke describes Mary, in his typically restrained prose, as "a virgin betrothed to a man named Joseph, of the house of David." To this brief description much needs to be added, and here tradition helps us. Mary was more than a virgin in fact. She had *vowed* herself to perpetual virginity. This led her to select Joseph from among her suitors and formally promise herself to him in the ceremony of betrothal. For Joseph too had vowed his purity to God. In his tenderness and strength Mary found the ideal protector for the life she designed to live.

We need not believe that Mary knew before the Annunciation exactly what God's plan for her was. It is clear from the New Testament narratives that God enlightened Mary by degrees and events, as her life unfolded. The central fact is that she had placed herself in God's hands for His purposes.

In picturing Mary to our minds and hearts we are rich in resources. Our Lord was "the most beautiful of the sons of men." He took his flesh from Mary, so we may well believe that she too was lovely beyond compare. *The Canticle of Canticles* prophesies of her, among other things, that "she is the lily of the lilies of the valley." As Our Lord was beautiful in a manly way, so was Our Lady beautiful—and she was all vowed to God, God inwrought to the core of her soul by prayer and thinking. She waited, in her perfection, for the visit of the angel.

According to the Scriptures, God has various ways of making known his will to human beings. Sometimes He sends a message in a dream or vision. Sometimes He leaves the announcement to His prophets. On great occasions He sends one of His angels.

Great art has portrayed angels with wings, but those spoken of in Scripture had the outward appearance of men, and nothing is mentioned about wings. Yet there must have been something about them—unearthly beauty, a look of commanding intelligence, some such quality—that made people realize at once what they were, that what they said was worthy of instant belief.

And so the angel Gabriel appeared in Nazareth in the beautiful spring-time, and came to Mary's house. St. Luke tells us that he "entered in," but he does not say where the angel found Mary. Perhaps she was at prayer, leaning on one of the little prayer-desks that were family heirlooms. Perhaps the angel found her at one of her household tasks, for prayers and work are eminently compatible, as cloistered nuns and monks know so well.

I like to think that, whether at work or at prayer, Gabriel found Mary in her garden. Eastern houses, in the days in which Our Lady lived, usually had a courtyard or a walled garden which was the center of family life in all the good months of the year. And somehow a garden fits the event in which paradise is once again opened to mankind.

Suddenly the angel is standing there before her like a flash of sunlight. His voice salutes her with an unexpected greeting.

"Hail, full of grace, the Lord is with thee."

The salutation is at once unexpected and strange. If the angel found Mary full of grace, then we can only infer that she was not only gracious and graceful but untouched by sin of any kind. To God's gaze even the smallest flaw shows, even the slightest stain. But here was one overflowing with grace, the matchless woman promised in the dawn of the world. For long ago, when Adam and Eve had been banished from the Garden of Eden, God promised a woman whose heel should crush a serpent.[1] This ancient promise was re-newed again in all the prophecies concerning the Messias.

Everything leads us to believe that the angel's greeting amazed Mary. A shadow of alarm must have moved across her face. She seemed so small to her own mind, in which God was all, and all beside Him littleness. Why should one come from God to her with such a flattering greeting?

The angel hastened to reassure Mary.

"Fear not, Mary, for thou hast found favor before God. And behold, thou shalt conceive in thy womb and shalt bring forth a son; and thou shalt call His name Jesus. He shall be great, and shall be called the Son of the

[1] Douay Version.

Most High; and the Lord God shall give to Him the throne of David His father, and He shall reign over the house of Jacob forever, and of His reign there shall be no end."

The stunning fact was clear. She had been chosen to be the mother of the Saviour, of Jesus the flower of Jesse's stem!

Here again was trouble for Mary's mind, since human flowering—the fruit of the womb—comes from man and woman. But Mary and her vow were wedded. God in her mind and heart was all, leaving no room for man. That was why her lips trembled to question,

"How shall this thing be, seeing that I know not man?"

Once again the angel was quick to give reassurance in the completion of his revelation.

"The Holy Spirit shall come upon thee, and the might of the Most High shall overshadow thee. Therefore the holy one to be begotten shall be called the Son of God. And behold Elizabeth, thy kinswoman, she also hath conceived a son in her old age, and she who was called barren is in her sixth month; for 'naught shall be impossible with God'."

The proof was there in the angel's words for Mary's mind and heart to measure with holy fear and trembling. Elizabeth, the childless one, and now long past the age to bear a child, would yet bring forth a son, for naught was impossible with God. Surely if God could make this come to pass, then just as surely could *virgin* and *mother* be equated, with both preserved intact.

Long ago, in her first childhood, Mary had bound herself to God. God's will, once known, was law, in which her mind and heart moved to a surrender thrilling in its modesty, monumental in its completeness:

"Behold the handmaid of the Lord; be it done to me according to thy word."

So God, through Mary, speaks to us in this first mystery of the rosary. She was the first in the Gospel story, as St. Luke shows, whose surrender to the will of God was total and complete.

"Thy kingdom come! Thy will be done!" So prayed Our Lord; so we must pray if we are to find His will and follow it. God's kingdom will not come to us unless we first give our wills to God. And not to be outdone,

God takes our gift and sends it back to us inestimably magnified and enriched in His indwelling Spirit, bringing us joy and peace that the world can never take away.

> Teach us the will's surrender, blessed Mother!
> Guide us on tranquil ways that lead to love!
> *Now* and at the hour of our death!

THE SECOND

JOYFUL MYSTERY

The Visitation

"Now in these days Mary arose and went with haste into the hill-country, to a town of Judah. And she entered the home of Zachary and saluted Elizabeth." LUKE I, 39-41.

We are told by St. Luke that Our Lady "arose and went with haste." She was obviously eager to see her cousin, anxious to hear Elizabeth's story and share the happiness of her kinswoman.

It is some fifty miles from Nazareth to the village now called Ain Karim, where Elizabeth and Zachary probably had their home. In the days in which Mary lived, such a journey entailed considerable labor and preparation. Provisions must be packed for the trip. Likely as not, Mary saddled the family donkey to carry her things, and then, sometimes riding, sometimes walking, started up into the hills on her two- or three-day journey. St. Luke does not indicate that anyone accompanied Our Lady, so we must presume she made the journey alone.

Fifty miles on foot or donkey-back seems a long, slow trip to us in this age of speed. To Mary it would not have appeared so. She was young, and strong like most village girls. Walking long distances was an old story to her. Besides, she was traveling from the monotony of the plains, where she lived, up into the coolness of the hills.

It is easy to picture her enjoying the beauties of the scenes along the way as she rode the small donkey or walked over the rough trail.

Spring in the hills is lovely. All about her, nature sang of joy in Mary's heart. What wonders God had wrought! She was filled with the spirit of God. Before the angel came she had kept herself continually in God's presence by an act of mind, and His will had been her peace. But now the Holy Spirit had suffused her entire being. Her mind and soul were exalted as simply as the world was exalted into beauty under the stainless sky of spring and the sun that warmed every nook and cranny of the rocks.

Mary's joy was linked with her complete acceptance of God's will. In her own mind she called herself God's slave. Acceptance of His plan was joy enough, though all that was to come was hidden in the mist of years that God would show her when the revelation was complete.

There must have leaped into her mind phrases and ideas from the Temple, songs, the psalms she knew so well—"Only God is great . . . triumph depends upon His mercy . . . it because of this that humble souls truly rejoice . . . the proud are cast down . . . the mighty are dethroned . . . but God will lift up the lowly with His powerful arm."

She saw these things to be so true of both herself and Elizabeth. How long her cousin had sorrowed at the reproach of barrenness. A barren woman past the age for children, still she hoped in God. And God Who renews the earth, even as the spring Mary saw about her in bursting bud and flower, had brought life to Elizabeth, and she in her old age would bear a child of promise.

Perhaps there flashed into Mary's mind a song from the first Book of Kings. Anna, great Samuel's mother, bearing a child when past the age, had praised God in these inspired words:

"My heart hath rejoiced in the Lord, and my horn is exalted in my God: my mouth is enlarged over my enemies, because I have joyed in Thy salvation.

"There is none holy as the Lord is: for there is no other beside Thee, and there is none strong like our God.

"Do not multiply to speak lofty things, boasting: let old matters depart from your mouth. For the Lord is a God of all knowledge, and to Him are thoughts prepared.

"The bow of the mighty is overcome: and the weak are girt with strength.

"They that were full before have hired out themselves for bread: and the hungry are filled; so that the barren hath borne many: and she that had many children is weakened.

"The Lord killeth and maketh alive: He bringeth down to hell and bringeth back again.

"The Lord maketh poor and maketh rich: He humbleth and He exalteth.

"He raiseth up the needy from the dust, and lifteth up the poor from the dunghill: that he may sit with princes, and hold the throne of glory. For the poles of the earth are the Lord's, and upon them He hath set the world.

"He will keep the feet of His saints, and the wicked shall be silent in darkness: because no man shall prevail by his own strength.

"The adversaries of the Lord shall fear Him: and upon them shall He thunder in the heavens. The Lord shall judge the ends of the earth; and He shall give empire to His King, and shall exalt the horn of His Christ." I KINGS II, 1-10.[1]

It was her happiness for another that hurried Mary's feet and made the slow hours like a dream of joy. Elizabeth was dear to her—now doubly dear after the angel's message.

So the days of travel passed, and the nights on the way, most likely spent with kinfolk. In their homes Mary knew the welcome of bread broken in joy and kindly love like a reflex of the love that leaped within her.

The long journey seemed a little thing when she saw the town of her desire in the distance, set in the saddle of green-brown hills—Ain Karim. It was golden with sunlight. White houses were bowered in olive trees and flowering locusts, dropping fragrance. And there in the midst was the house of Zachary and Elizabeth, asleep in the sun.

Our Lady tied the donkey in the shade where grass was plentiful. Forgetting all else she hurried forward, and pushed aside the leather curtain of the door. At first her sun-dazed eyes must have been blinded by the inner gloom. Then, at last, she saw Elizabeth—sitting alone, and big with child. Beyond her was the garden-courtyard.

"Elizabeth!" The greeting startled the seated woman. Then, when she saw who it was that called, the heavy figure swiftly rose. There was a long embrace. Tears of joy were on their cheeks. Suddenly the room seemed lit with fire from above, and heavenly knowledge poured into Elizabeth's mind so that she cried out with a loud voice,

"Blessed art thou among women, and blessed is the fruit of thy womb!

[1] Douay Version.

And whence this to me that the mother of my Lord should come unto me?

"For behold, when the sound of thy salutation fell on mine ears the babe in my womb leapt with gladness. And blessed art thou who hast believed, for what the Lord hath promised thee shall be accomplished."

Now Mary saw a step even beyond the promise of the angel's words to her, in the inspired greeting of Elizabeth. Lowliness was raised from the dust to flower. The barren would bloom and God be magnified in both of them. Song that was food for meditation all the way from Nazareth sprang to Mary's lips in joy, in exaltation. And Mary said:

> *"My soul doth magnify the Lord,*
> *and my spirit hath exulted in God my Saviour,*
> *Because He hath regarded the lowliness of His handmaid:*
> *yea, behold, henceforth all generations shall call me*
> *blessed:*
> *Because He who is mighty hath wrought great things for*
> *me,*
> *and holy is His name:*
> *And for generation upon generation is His mercy, unto*
> *them that fear Him.*
> *He hath put forth His arm powerfully:*
> *He hath scattered the proud in their heart's conceit:*
> *He hath cast down monarchs from their thrones,*
> *and the lowly He hath exalted.*
> *He hath filled the hungry with good things,*
> *and the rich He hath sent away empty.*
> *He hath come to the aid of Israel, His servant,*
> *mindful of His mercy*
> *(Even as He promised unto our fathers)*
> *to Abraham and to his seed for ever."*
>
> LUKE I, 46-55.

This mystery shows us how beautiful it is to think of others. When Gabriel told Mary that Elizabeth would bear a child in her old age, Our Lady was so delighted that she rose up at once and went *in haste* into the hill country where Elizabeth lived. Like all generous souls, she wanted to be the first to congratulate Elizabeth, and Mary alone knew that this was a special favor of God linked with her own high destiny.

It was quite natural that Mary's mind, as she journeyed toward Elizabeth's house, should have been busy with passages from the psalms and the Old Testament which spoke of God and His kindness toward those who trust in Him. Like all well-trained Hebrew girls of her time, Mary knew the Scriptures well and had memorized many passages from them, especially those, we may well believe, that memorialized God's goodness to the women of Israel. The song of Anna, after the birth of Samuel, was particularly apropos, since it summed up another case just like Elizabeth's.

Mary's delight in Elizabeth's good fortune had little thought of self in it. And, when the two women met, God was pleased to glorify Mary's selflessness and humility in the greeting she received. It is obvious that Elizabeth was inspired by the Holy Spirit to know that Mary had been chosen to bear the long-expected Messias. That is why she cried out "Blessed art thou among women, and blessed is the fruit of thy womb! And whence this to me that the mother of my Lord should come unto me?"

Transfigured with joy and astonishment that Elizabeth knew all the angel had foretold, Mary burst into a poem of praise that speaks the joy of both women. The words and phrases she used were from the holy books she knew so well, but in these circumstances, they made a superb new poem that will thrill all humanity to the end of time. God is great. All else is little. When littleness sees and admits its dependence on God, then God is kind. God will humble the proud, but the humble shall be exalted even as Mary and Elizabeth were, because of their loving dependence on Him. In this way God fulfills the ancient promise made to Abraham and his people.

Teach us, holy Mary, how great God is, how small we are. Teach us to love God for Himself. Teach us to see His beauty shining in the human faces all about us. So, from you, we learn to think first of God—and neighbor next—before we think of self. Now and at the hour of our death. Amen.

THE THIRD

JOYFUL MYSTERY

The Birth of Our Lord

"Now it came to pass that in those days there went forth an edict from Caesar Augustus for the registration of the whole world. The first registration occurred when Quirinius was governor of Syria. So all went to enregister themselves, every man to his own town. And Joseph likewise went up from Galilee into Judaea, from the town of Nazareth to the town of David which is called Bethlehem—for he was of the house and family of David—to enregister himself together with Mary his betrothed, who was with child. And it came to pass that whilst they were there she completed the days of her delivery and brought forth her first-born son; and she swathed Him round and laid Him in a manger, because there was no place for them in the inn." LUKE II, 1-7.

With characteristic simplicity and restraint, St. Luke tells us of the events so dear to all who love Christmas. He first gives us two historical references which date and frame his memorable story, so that we may see where it belongs in the long panorama of time and that we may also realize we are dealing with actual history.

Caesar Augustus was the supreme ruler of the Roman Empire between 27 B.C. and A.D. 14. This first Roman emperor was a great builder, and he constantly needed huge sums of money for his many building projects which practically remade the face of Rome. Augustus was also a reformer, and the census taken at the time Our Lord was born may well have been decreed as part of the emperor's reform of taxes and the civil service. It was probably for this reason that he ordered the whole Roman world to be enrolled for tax purposes—the enrollment of which St. Luke speaks.

Luke's second historical reference is still more precise. We are told the first tax enrollment was made while Quirinius was governor of Syria. Quirinius was twice governor of Syria, once in conjunction with Sentius Saturninius and once by himself at a later date, 9 B.C.-A.D. 6. Judea was one of the provinces of Syria.

Herod was king of Judea, and it is likely that the census in Palestine was made under his direction and was supervised by Jewish officials. Since the Jews were organized by families and tribes it was necessary for Joseph to go to the chief city of his tribe, which was Bethlehem. It was King David's town, and because Joseph was one of David's descendants he had to go to David's town to register.

Mary went along with him to be registered. She too was of David's line. There was another reason for her going with Joseph, in that she was heavy with child and the hour for her delivery was at hand. It may seem odd to us today that Joseph should have taken the risk of the Child's being born far away from home in circumstances that might be beyond his control. We live in a time when babies are normally born in aseptic hospitals, under a doctor's careful supervision. But in Joseph's day children were born wherever the family chanced to be, with or without supervision, except for an occasional midwife.

Besides, the Scriptures had foretold that the Messias would be born in Bethlehem of Judea. Joseph and Mary, then, must have been moved by the Holy Spirit to go to Bethlehem in the serene confidence that the Child would be born there according to the promise. It appears that Mary had taken the swaddling bands with her in preparation for the great event. She must have been certain that her baby would be born on this journey.

Tradition tells us that the trip from Nazareth was made with the aid of the family donkey. Great artists have given us many charming variations of the theme. St. Joseph would have led the donkey, with Mary riding behind, transfigured with the joy so soon to come into the world. The donkey also served another purpose, that of carrying simple household effects to make life along the way more bearable, the personal baggage of Mary and Joseph, and the various things necessary for the birth and care of a newborn child.

Once again they went along through the hill tracks, perhaps the same paths that had taken Mary to Ain Karim and Elizabeth. It would have been possible to stay overnight with relatives or old friends. Hospitality in those days was the unwritten law of the land, even as it is today in the East. But it was a test of Mary's and Joseph's faith and constancy that, once in Bethlehem, they found the village inn, and doubtless every village home, crowded with the throngs of David's descendants who had come themselves to register. At first it must have been a shock to discover that there was no room for them in the inn or in the houses of the village.

In looking back from our vantage point, however, we can see the finger of God in this circumstance. The village inns of Our Lord's day in Palestine were crudely roofed shelters, little more than sheds, built around a large central courtyard in which the beasts of burden could be tethered for safe keeping. Inns were noisy, not very clean, and often occupied by people as sinful and careless as ourselves. In a sense, then, it was not fitting that the Son of God should have been born in such tawdry circumstances and with such complete lack of privacy and genuine dignity.

How Joseph found the stable-cave that tradition points out as Our Lord's birthplace we do not know, but if we picture it as the large room tradition says it was, and think of it as being filled with sweet-smelling hay, we can see that it was a much more dignified and private place for a child to be born than the dirty, crowded inn, with its courtyard filled with braying donkeys and stinking camels. When the lamps Joseph carried with him were lighted and the darkness of the cave was dispelled, it must have seemed snug and cozy in contrast to the cold of the night outside. Perhaps warm woven rugs were spread out on the hay, while, after a simple supper, they waited with mounting joy for the birth of Mary's Child.

That event for which the world had waited so long is described by St. Luke with delicacy and simplicity: "she completed the days of her delivery and brought forth her first-born son; and she swathed Him round and laid Him in a manger. . . ."

Do such bare phrases speak of serenity and joy in the birth of the Child? I think they do. And the Church tells us that the birth of the Son of God was not only painless and filled with joy, but that Mary still remained a virgin. Surely these things are not astonishing in any way. God Who made the world could make His Son's entrance into the world a complete joy in every circumstance. The pains of birth are one of the punishments of original sin. Mary being sinless was exempt from them.

But what indescribable happiness must have flooded Mary when she first looked on her newborn Son! What Gabriel had told her of her Child's destiny had prepared her to see Him as a great king some day. Now as she looked at Him in those first moments He seemed a king indeed—king of her heart and fit to charm the hearts of a whole world. And surely angels must have been there, whether visible in their blinding brightness or not, as they looked upon their God.

It is easy enough for us to imagine these things, because though St. Luke treats the actual birth of Our Lord with reverent restraint, he returns at once to the high atmosphere of wonder in which his story is being told:

"And in the same district were shepherds living out in the fields and keeping the night-watches over their flock. And an angel of the Lord stood by them, and the glory of the Lord shone about them, and they feared with a great fear. And the angel said to them, 'Fear not, for behold, I bring you glad tidings of a great joy which shall be to all the people; for there hath been born to you this day a saviour, who is Christ the Lord, in the town of David. And this shall be to you a sign thereof: ye shall find a babe enswathed and lying in a manger.'

"And suddenly there appeared with the angel a multitude of the heavenly host praising God and saying 'Glory to God in the highest, and peace upon earth among men of his good pleasure!'

"And it came to pass that when the angels had departed from them into heaven, the shepherds said one to another, 'Let us go, then, to Bethlehem and see this thing which has come to pass, which the Lord hath made known to us.'

"So they went with haste and found Mary and Joseph, and the babe lying in a manger. And when they had seen, they made known what had been told them concerning this child. And all that heard marvelled at what was told them by the shepherds. But Mary stored up all these things in her heart and pondered them.

"And the shepherds returned, glorifying and praising God for all that they had heard and had seen, even as had been told them." LUKE II, 8-20.

The lives of shepherds in ancient times were rough and difficult. They lived mostly in the open, following their flocks over hills and plains, watching them and caring for them with fidelity and skill, which evokes in our minds the image of the Good Shepherd which Our Lord later applied to Himself. The Pharisees tended to despise shepherds because, working seven days a week as shepherds did, they were unable to observe all the exacting precepts of the rabbinical law. But God, Who knows and judges hearts, picked shepherds for the first public revelation of the Incarnation.

Perhaps we can see a little into God's reasons. First of all, the shepherds were simple men. Simplicity does not rule out wisdom. Men who know nature and live in the open have astonishing knowledge of their world. Lonely and often silent through the heat of the day and nights heavy with stars, they come to live by intuition and the heart. In their long silences they come to appreciate the beauty of the world about them, and in doing so learn to appreciate the beauty of God and all the unseen wonders of the universe.

Simple as they were, and uncomplex, the blinding light and the glory about them in the midnight plain filled them with the fear which is the beginning of wisdom. In mind and soul they were made ready to drink in the revelation of the Saviour, born at last into the world, and they were the first ones noted in Scripture to hear the angels singing.

> *"Glory to God in the highest*
> *And peace on earth to men of good will."*

Men of good will are men of love. Their love of God moves out radiantly upon all mankind. These shepherds, so tender toward their charges, so solicitous of the young lambs, were indeed men of good will and compassion. It was their good will, too, which stirred them into action. They were anxious to see this wonder that had come to pass. Leaving some of their number in charge of the flock they went to Bethlehem and found Mary and Joseph and the Child.

It was to Mary that they told the full story of God's revelation to them, and she "stored up all these things in her heart and pondered them," an indication to us that St. Luke may have heard the story of Our Lord's birth from Our Lady herself.

The rich detail clustered about this mystery of the rosary is not yet complete. It is to be presumed that the shepherds who were the first to hear the glad tidings were Jews. But the Incarnation was meant to touch all men. Christ was the new Adam and all men were His sons. This part of the

Christmas story is not found in St. Luke's account. For it we must turn to the Gospel of St. Matthew.

"Now when Jesus was born in Bethlehem of Judaea in the days of King Herod, behold, there came Magi from the East to Jerusalem, saying, 'Where is He that hath been born king of the Jews? For we have seen His star in the East and are come to worship Him.'

"Upon hearing this, King Herod was troubled, and all Jerusalem with him. And he gathered together all the high priests and scribes of the people, and enquired of them where the Christ was to be born. And they said to him, 'In Bethlehem of Judaea; for so it is written through the prophet:

> And thou, Bethlehem, land of Judah,
> art no wise least among the rulers of Judah;
> For from thee shall come forth a ruler,
> who shall tend my people Israel.

"Then Herod called the Magi secretly and learned from them the exact time when the star had appeared. And sending them to Bethlehem, he said, 'Go, and make careful enquiry concerning the child, and when ye have found him let me know, that I too may come and worship him.'

"So after hearing the King they departed; and behold, the star which they had seen in the East moved on before them till it came to rest over the spot where was the child. And on seeing the star they rejoiced with exceeding great joy. And entering the house, they saw the child with Mary His mother, and falling down they worshipped Him. And they opened their treasures and offered Him gifts, gold and frankincense and myrrh. And being warned in a dream not to return to Herod, they withdrew to their own country by another way." MATTHEW II, 1-12.

Like St. Luke, Matthew starts his account of the first gentiles to see our Lord with a historical reference to Herod, so-called the Great, King of Judea at the time of Our Lord's birth. Actually, as we shall see from what follows, Herod was a cruel despot who would resort to any means in order to maintain his power or popularity.

The Magi, it is thought, were from a priestly tribe of Medes living south of the Jordan River. Their history was connected with the study of the stars and foretelling the future. In the case of these particular Magi, St. Matthew obviously thinks of them as being first of all men of good will and spiritual depth, having some tradition that the king of the world was to be born when certain stars were in conjunction. When they saw the great star blazing in the east they knew the time was at hand. Probably they presumed that all men would be glad to see such a king and, knowing He was to be born in Israel, they came to King Herod in order to get the information which would take them to the Child by the shortest route.

St. Matthew says King Herod was troubled, as was all Jerusalem. This implies that all the people of Jerusalem had seen the great star in the sky and wondered what it meant—good or evil. When Herod learned from the Magi that the star was the star of the newborn king of the Jews he trembled. There would be but one so-styled, and that was the long-expected Messias. That was why Herod asked the priests and the scribes where "the Christ" was to be born. They answered, "In Bethlehem."

The crafty king then called in the Magi and asked them the exact time when the great star first appeared. With this information he hoped to be able to estimate just how old his rival was. To make doubly sure, Herod asked the Magi to make careful inquiry about the Child in order to be more certain he would be able to kill the right boy. Herod's statement that he wished to "worship the Child," once the Magi had found him, seemed to the wise men to be made in good faith.

So the Magi departed from Jerusalem. Now in the same wondrous way the star moved out of its fixed position and by its light led the way to the very spot where the Child was.

St. Matthew says the Magi entered the *house* where the Child was. Does the word *house* mean that the Holy Family had moved from the stable cave? Since we do not know the precise time of the wise men's visit we do not know for certain exactly where in Bethlehem the Magi visited the Holy Family. We do know that they "fell down and adored" the Child, which was their homage paid to God. The offering of incense is further confirmation that they knew the Child was God.

Having been "warned in a dream" not to return to Herod, they took one of the lesser-known roads and returned home in secret.

Joseph, too, was warned by an angel that Herod threatened the life of Jesus, and the angel commanded Joseph to take the Child and His mother to Egypt, where they remained until the death of Herod.

Having been thwarted by the Magi and not knowing that the Holy

Family was already safe in Egypt, Herod tried to make certain that he would destroy his rival. So he sent his soldiers to kill all male children who were less than two years old.

That is the Christmas story, as told in the Scriptures. A journey is taken, a child is born, an angelic revelation is made to Jewish shepherds, a star appears, gentile wise men follow it and adore a King. It is all simply told, as we find it in the Gospels, but the Incarnation is so important to humanity that men through the ages have pondered it lovingly. The most superb artists have delighted in painting it in colors of their own exuberant fancy. The stable becomes something of a palace, the shepherds are turned into idealized courtiers, the Magi are transformed into kings with royal trappings and retinues of servants. Even names have been invented for the royal visitors: Caspar, Melchior and Balthasar. One of them is ultimately pictured as a black man indicating that where love is, race is inconsequential and that all men are of equal value in the sight of God.

The Incarnation is *God with us*. It means God with us not as a stranger but as one of us, wearing our flesh, knowing our daily sorrows and joys.

Mothers are beautiful and babies are dear to all normal human beings, but through this great Mother and the birth of her Child the gates of heaven are opened and a supernatural Eden is once again created for the joy and salvation of men. Mary is the new Eve, but in her the will is not in the least rebellious. It is wedded to God's will in perfect harmony.

O Mary, great Mother of God, teach us to see how joyous it is to have God with us in the Mass and Sacraments, in the Church and in the dwelling of the Holy Spirit in our hearts. Make each day a Christmas in our hearts. Help us to grow as simple as shepherds, as generous in wisdom and love as kings. Keep us ever with Him, now and at the hour of our death.

THE FOURTH

JOYFUL MYSTERY

The Presentation

" And when 'their days of purification had been completed' according to the Law of Moses, they brought Him up to Jerusalem to present Him to the Lord, as it is written in the Law of the Lord, 'Every male that openeth the womb shall be called holy to the Lord'; and to offer for sacrifice, according to what is said in the Law of the Lord, 'a pair of turtle-doves or two young pigeons.' " LUKE II, 22-24.

The fourth joyful mystery is for many people a difficult subject for proper meditation because it requires precise information and graphic detail for its correct visualization.

We know from St. Matthew's Gospel that after the visit of the Magi to Bethlehem, St. Joseph was warned in a dream that Herod menaced the life of the Child. Joseph was told to go to Egypt and he took Mary and the Child there until the death of Herod, after which they returned to their house in Nazareth.

St. Luke has nothing to say about the flight into Egypt, very probably because St. Matthew had already told that story from the childhood of Jesus. What, then, was the time relationship between the presentation, the visit of the Magi, and the flight into Egypt?

Since St. Luke states very clearly that the Holy Family went to Jerusalem for the presentation when their "purification had been completed," we begin to have a very definite indication of the correct sequence of these events.

The purification for a Jewish woman after the birth of a male child was thirty-three days. Bethlehem is only about six miles from Jerusalem, and it would have been easy to go up to the temple for presentation of the Child and return to David's town the same day. Obviously, it must have been after Our Lord's presentation that the visit of the wise men took place, with the flight into Egypt following soon after.

The presentation of every male child to God was commanded by the Law of Moses. Certainly such presentation was unnecessary in Our Lord's case, just as there was no need for Our Lady to undergo the thirty-three days of ritual purification. But Our Lord said of Himself that He came to fulfill the law and not to abolish it, and the Blessed Virgin was equally eager to do everything commanded by the law of her people.

The temple to which Mary took Jesus was the center of Jerusalem and the very heart of the Jewish people. When most people think of the temple in Our Lord's time, they think of Solomon's temple, which had been completely destroyed by the Babylonians centuries before Christ was born. Various makeshift temples had been erected on the same spot on top of Mt. Moriah, but it was not until the Romans named Herod the Great as king of Judea in 37 B.C., that a new temple worthy of God came to be built on God's holy mountain.

Herod, who was noted for his insane pride, was clearly determined to outdo Solomon's effort. The measurements of Solomon's temple and a fairly complete description of it were set down in the third book of Kings and were well known to every Jew. By outdoing Solomon in the new building, Herod could at once satisfy his own pride and earn the gratitude of all his people.

In preparation for the building, a much larger area was leveled off on the top of the mountain and buttressed with walls of beautifully cut stone. A thousand priests were carefully trained in the various necessary crafts, and the building was started in 20 B.C. Though Herod's magnificently ambitious plan was not to be finished until A.D. 64, its fabric was largely complete at the time of the presentation, and it was already known as one of the seven wonders of the antique world.

It was to this superb building that Our Lady, carrying Jesus in her arms, came on that wintry day long ago. Our Lady's heart must have been bursting with joy, as she and Joseph ascended the sacred mountain, to realize that it was to be her privilege in her offering on this day to give God back His Son in human guise. It was at once a joyful and solemn occasion.

Above them on the mountain loomed the various levels of the temple. The large court of the gentiles in which unbelievers might show themselves was on the first level. The women's court was on the level above the gentiles' court. From the women's area, a flight of fifteen semicircular steps, crowned with a carved gate, known as the Beautiful Gate, led to the courtyard of the men. In the midst of this courtyard stood the altar of incense and the carved bronze lavers or baths, holding water for priestly ablutions.

Beyond the court of the men and half surrounded by it was the center of the holy place—the house in which God dwelt. It was divided into two sections. The larger of these areas held the golden tables of bread, altars of incense and seven-branched lights. Beyond it, marked off by a rainbow-colored curtain of woven cotton and silk, was the sacred spot reserved for the glory of God. The high priest alone was permitted entrance into this holy place once each year. It was finished throughout with gold and rose to a cubed pinnacle that on its outer surface reflected the light with flashing splendor.

When we think of courts today we think of them as open spaces. The courts of the temple were open in the center, with arcades and rooms on their sides supported on forests of pillars of polished marble in various colors. The porch of King Herod, which looked down on the main part of Jerusalem, was particularly splendid. Its ranks of double Ionic pillars were some fifty feet high. Above them the lesser pillars of the higher courts showed, and beyond these the marble of the holy place, carved and gilded, all dominated by the cube of the holy of holies like a golden finger pointing to the sky.

In the rooms built into the walls of the building lived the priests on duty. There were also storerooms for the wheat and oil and places where pilgrims could buy animals for the sacrifices of lambs and sheep, oxen and doves. There were halls for debate and the training of the temple singers, libraries of books and many other rooms serving the complex routine of daily worship and Jewish life.

According to the law, the first-born son belonged to God and had to be offered to God in sacrifice, in memory of the fact that He had spared the first-born of Jewish families on the night of the first Passover. But the child could be brought back from God by the offering of five shekels of silver and the substitution of a lamb for sacrifice. If the parents of the child were too poor to afford these gifts, they were permitted to offer a pair of turtle doves or two young pigeons.

Coming through the carved and towering gate of the gentiles' court, Mary and Joseph would have stopped to buy their turtle doves for sacrifice. Looking at these gentle creatures in their wicker cages, Mary may well have thought of their resemblance to the Child, so warm and quiet in her arms. He too was like a dove, so gentle and so innocent. Hers was the "poor woman's sacrifice," but it was a fitting one in that it matched the sweet gentleness of her Child.

Once in the women's court, the Holy Family found themselves in the midst of groups of devout women worshippers dressed in their best clothes, as we are today when we go to worship God. On all sides were shining pillars ornamented with golden capitals. At the top of the fifteen semicircular steps leading to the men's court loomed the wonder of the Beautiful Gate, with its foliated carving. Its gold- and silver-plated doors were folded back. In the open space of this gold and silver frame could be seen the altar of sacrifice, smoking continually in the clear morning air. Probably Joseph went into the men's court to find one of the priests on duty, to whom he could present the doves for sacrifice.

We can see them standing there so clearly—the lovely Mother and her lovely Child. All the glories offered to God, of gold and silver, of marble and carved stone, surrounded them with a background of splendor. But better than this ranked magnificence were the gifts offered by Mary: her own virginal heart, and her Son, Whose baby fingers were capable of opening the gates of eternal life to all men.

What Mary's prayer to God was like we do not know, but we do know that she proved herself an excellent poet in the *Magnificat,* and that she knew all the lovely phrases from the holy books in which God had been praised by the poets and prophets from time immemorial.

That there must have been something inexpressibly and significantly beautiful in the little group St. Luke indicates quite clearly: "And behold, there was in Jerusalem a man named Symeon (Simeon), and this man was just and devout, awaiting the consolation of Israel, and the Holy Spirit was upon him; and it had been revealed to him by the Holy Spirit that he should not see death before he had seen the Christ of the Lord. And he came in the Spirit to the temple; and when the parents brought in the child Jesus, to carry out the custom of the Law in His regard, himself also received Him into his arms and blessed God and said:

> 'Now Thou dost dismiss Thy servant, O Master,
>   according to Thy word, in peace;
> Because mine eyes have seen Thy salvation,
>   which Thou hast prepared before the face of all the
>   peoples:
> A light of revelation unto the gentiles,
>   and of glory for Thy people Israel.' "
>   LUKE II, 25-32.

In the midst of all the women and men gathered in the women's court for the same purpose for which Mary and Joseph had come, Symeon was inspired to single out the Holy Family. And taking the Child into his arms, Symeon broke into a poem of joy that his dim old eyes had at last seen the Redeemer Who would be the glory and salvation of all men, whether Jew or gentile—the salvation of God!

St. Luke proceeds to tell us that "His father and mother marvelled at the things that were said concerning Him." Here again the picture is a memorable one. All parents who have children delight in hearing them praised, and Mary and Joseph must have listened with delight to the amazing tribute to the Infant. This venerable stranger helped Mary to see more clearly into the revelation God had made to her, either directly, through the angel, or through other people, such as Elizabeth and the shepherds.

With grateful hearts she and Joseph received the blessing of Symeon, and Mary must obviously have been surprised when Symeon spoke to her directly: "Behold, this Child is set for the fall and for the rise of many in Israel, and for a sign that shall be contradicted—yea, and thine own soul a sword shall pierce—that the thoughts of many hearts may be revealed." LUKE II, 34-35.

In his words to Our Lady, though they are hidden in the generalities of prophecy, Symeon had forecast the whole course of Christ's life. Many in Israel would rise to a new life through Him, many like Judas and the high priests would tumble to degradation, and the same may be said of ourselves today. The sign that He was, and the signs of His miracles, even His resurrection, would be denied and reasoned away. His suffering and death would pierce the heart of Mary with a great sword of sorrow, so that through Him and her many hearts should be moved to declare themselves, either for or against Christ and His revelations.

The encounter with Symeon had been an extraordinary one, marking this day of presentation forever in Mary's mind. Almost before she could savor it fully, it was enlarged and made more memorable by a second person: "And there was Anna, a prophetess, daughter of Phanuel, of the tribe of Asher; she was far advanced in age, and had lived with her husband seven years from her maidenhood, and as a widow to eighty-four years. She departed not from the temple, with fastings and prayers worshipping day and night. And at that same hour she came upon them and returned thanks to God, and she spoke of the Child to all that were awaiting the redemption of Jerusalem." LUKE II, 36-38.

Again St. Luke gives us an unforgettable picture. Anna, we are informed, is venerable like Symeon. She has so loved God and His house that she has served Him and prayed to Him night and day for many years since she became a widow. She is also a prophetess who foretells the future.

We can easily picture her coming along through the court of women, picking her way through the crowd. Suddenly she stops before Mary and Joseph, looks into the shining face of Jesus and, like Symeon, she too gives thanks for seeing the Saviour. Then, knowing the temple and its worshippers well, as she does from seeing them day after day through the years, Anna tells them the good news that the redemption of Israel is at hand.

In this mystery of the rosary we learn how to serve God with joy in big and little things. Mary had no need to be purified; she was purity itself. Yet she waited out the days of her purification because it was in the law of her people.

Christ had no need to be presented to His Father; but the law of Moses said the firstborn must be presented to God and brought back. Since it was the law, Mary complied.

Her compliance was not made with grumbling and reluctance; she followed the commands of Moses with joy. She was happy to go up to the temple, happy to present her Child to God.

Teach us your happiness in serving God and His laws, holy Mother. Teach us to love His house. Help us to keep from complaining against the laws of God and His Church. Help us to serve God with joy. Strengthen us in following minutely all that we are commanded to do in His name, now and at the hour of our death.

THE FIFTH

JOYFUL MYSTERY

The Finding of the Child Jesus in the Temple

" AND the child grew and waxed strong, filled with wisdom, and the grace of God was upon Him.

"And His parents were wont to go every year to Jerusalem at the feast of the passover. And when He was twelve years old, they went up according to the practice of the feast; and when they had fulfilled the days and were returning, the boy Jesus remained in Jerusalem, and His parents knew it not. Thinking that He was in the caravan, they came a day's journey, and sought for Him among their kinsfolk and acquaintance, and since they found Him not, they returned to Jerusalem in search of Him." LUKE II, 40-45.

The Gospels are mostly silent about the childhood of Jesus. In speaking here of that period of Our Lord's life, St. Luke does so with restraint and compression but in his account we can find several significant things.

First of all, we see that Jesus was a normal, healthy boy: handsome, sturdy, active and full of the joy of life. A regular boy loves to walk and swim and climb trees, play games and make excursions into interesting places in his home neighborhood. We may presume, from St. Luke's words, that Our Lord grew up in this way.

Nazareth was a country town where everyone knew all his neighbors. To the north and west of the town stretched the great plain of Esdraleon. Walking through it, Jesus learned to see into all those rich simplicities of life which

He later used with telling effect in His parables. The lilies of the field, the good shepherd tenderly watching over his sheep, the birds of the air singing in the locust trees, the gleaning of the burnt-gold fields after the wheat had been gathered—it was all there about Him in Nazareth, while He was growing up.

Tradition asserts that Jesus early learned to help Joseph with his carpentry, and this too is quite likely. Children in the ancient days came to responsibility early, like pioneer children of the United States. It is easy to picture Jesus learning to handle saw and chisel and broadaxe until he was expert in their use and strong from labor as well as play. Only too often we forget that manual labor is holy. St. Joseph, the Blessed Virgin, and Our Lord all worked with their hands. The holiest saints were not afraid to follow their example. That is why the monks always said, "To labor is to pray."

But there must have been something about Jesus which marked Him off from the ordinary crowd of children. St. Luke says he was "filled with wisdom and the grace of God was upon Him." And the Church teaches us that the fullness of spiritual wisdom was with Jesus from the very beginning because He was the Son of God. But He was also man. Like all of us He had to accumulate His human skills and wisdom from daily experience and instruction. We may be sure that Mary and Joseph helped Him with these things. Yet some of the plenitude of God's grace within Him must have shone forth for all to see.

St. Luke lets us know, too, that their family life was not a narrow one. As the winter sky lightened toward spring, the Holy Family looked forward to their annual excursion to Jerusalem, much as we would look forward to a trip to Rome.

For a little while the country ways and manners of Nazareth would be put aside in the big city that Jerusalem was. During the great feast of the Pasch the population of Jerusalem was swollen with pious Jews from all over the Roman Empire. They arrived in their thousands, wearing strange dress and bringing news from the whole civilized world.

In addition to these excitements there was for the Holy Family the joy of seeing God's house once again, the superb temple on the top of Mount Moriah, like a great white cloud, tinged with gold and the colors of sunset. The temple was still being built and ornamented year after year. As the Holy

Family went to worship they would have commented and exclaimed over the magnificent additions since their visit the year before.

Doubtless they sat down with friends or relations at the Paschal table crowned with unblemished lamb edged with bitter lettuce. The bread would be broken, the wine cup passed from hand to hand while they recounted the mercy of God in their deliverance from Egypt, and the many past glories of their people.

When Jesus prepared to go up to Jerusalem in his twelfth year the excitement must have been keener than usual. A boy about twelve was in the Jewish way of thinking already a man, mentally and physically. It would no longer be necessary for Him to go to the temple with the women. Now in His ritual cap and shawl He could follow His foster father into the court of the men. Now He was able to see closer and more intimately the altar of sacrifice smoking perpetually and all the holy things associated with the worship of His Father. Now He could wander at will to the larger rooms along the temple walls where the rabbis taught and argued over points of law or ceremonial. Or He could walk in the court of the gentiles among the money-changers, busy working out the percentages on money brought from all over the world, and the knots of merchants selling lambs and doves for sacrifice.

Starting out from their home in Nazareth, the Holy Family probably joined a pilgrim party from the village. Travel in groups was a protection against robbers. It was also more interesting than traveling alone. Very often the men would be in a group by themselves, setting the pace. The party of village women and children followed their men at a more leisurely pace until nightfall, when the two groups came together.

A caravan of this sort progressing through various villages along the way to Jerusalem was sure to be swelled by the constant addition of new groups of pilgrims. By the time the environs of Jerusalem were in sight the original small party might number several hundred people. Almost every family had a donkey or some sort of beast of burden, thus adding to the noise, confusion and general excitement.

The Jews celebrated their feast days from sundown to sundown. On the evening of the great feast of the Passover, Jerusalem would dramatically become hushed. All work would cease, the fires of thousands of hearths would be quenched, the streets would be deserted. A holy silence descended.

Within doors, families stood about the Paschal table. Their long gowns were girded up for flight, heavy sandals were on their feet and staves were in their hands, as they had been in that day long past when they awaited word from Moses that would take them out of Egypt forever. That first Passover had been a night of suspense and terror, for the avenging angel of the Lord was passing over Egypt killing the first-born of every family whose doorposts and lintel were unmarked with the blood of the Paschal lamb.

So solemn was this feast of the Passover that it lasted from the four-teenth day of Nisan to the twenty-first. No yeast was to be allowed in any Jewish home during that week, and all the people were to eat unleavened bread for the entire period. The Sabbath of the Passover and the Sabbath ending the week with the feast of unleavened bread were high holy days in which all work ceased and the people turned to prayer and the lessons of the holy books.

We may be sure that Our Lord gave Himself to the celebration of these feasts with all His heart. He was now a man standing before His Father, and the heart of Jesus must have yearned to begin the work for which He had come into the world.

When the holy days were over, with their solemn feasts and visits to God's house, the caravan going north to Nazareth had probably appointed a meeting place for the various parties before proceeding on their journey. It may well have been one of the north gates of the city.

Probably Mary and Joseph, because they respected the self-reliance of Jesus, and had high regard for His obedience to their wishes, made no at-tempt to inquire whether or not He had joined the caravan. They presumed He was there. In any event, they had traveled north for a day before they discovered Jesus was nowhere to be found among the various groups. This obviously alarmed them. With fear and sorrow filling their hearts they left the train and started back toward Jerusalem.

We may be sure that Mary was deeply troubled. Nothing in her life with Jesus had prepared her for this. She had always expected Him to do the cor-rect thing and He had never disappointed her. What could have happened to Him? Like all mothers, she must have imagined the worst. Maybe He was sick, or injured, or dead. Maybe He was somewhere on the road, hungry and tired, trying to find the caravan.

Upon reaching Jerusalem, Mary and Joseph probably spent most of the day trying to find some clue to the whereabouts of Jesus among their relations and friends in Jerusalem. Perhaps some one of these had seen the boy in the temple, or perhaps Mary knew from Jesus' love of the holy place that she was almost sure to find Him there.

"And it came to pass that after three days they found Him in the temple, seated in the midst of the teachers, both listening to them and asking them questions. And all that heard Him were amazed at His intelligence and His answers. And upon seeing Him they were struck with wonder; and His mother said unto Him, 'My Child, why hast Thou done so to us? Behold, Thy father and I seek Thee sorrowing.'

"And He said unto them, 'How is it that ye sought Me? Knew ye not that I must needs be in My Father's house?'

"And they understood not the word which He spoke to them.

"And He went down with them and came to Nazareth, and was subject to them. And His mother stored up all these things in her heart.

"And Jesus advanced in wisdom and age and grace before God and men." LUKE II, 46-52.

We can see the two distraught figures walking up to the holy place. Doubtless they first searched the court of the gentiles and the women's court; then Joseph went on to the men's court asking for some rumor of his foster-child. The search would not be easy in a place as vast as the temple, and still crowded with foreign visitors. Finally, in one of the great rooms reserved for public discussions, they found Him.

Learned doctors of the law of Moses had gathered in Jerusalem from all over the Roman Empire. They were famous men, enormously learned, who loved to argue over the fine points of the law and its meaning, and the visiting public was allowed to listen in on their long discussions. It must have amazed Mary to discover her Son, not standing on the sidelines, but seated among this august assembly as one of them. He was listening to them and asking questions, and astonishing the learned men with both His questions and answers. Mary and Joseph were "struck with wonder" at the sight.

They may have listened and watched Him for a while, filled with joy to see Him alive and well. Then, catching His eye or attracting His attention in some manner, they drew Him out of the room into one of the corridors or courts.

It was, then, in privacy that Mary probably voiced her reproachful questions, "My Child, why hast Thou done so to us? Behold, Thy father and I seek Thee sorrowing?"

The answer came with simple finality. "How is it that ye sought Me? Know ye not that I must needs be in My Father's house?"

There it was—the announcement of His person and His mission. God was His Father and He must do His Father's work.

Mary and Joseph clearly found it hard to understand the full meaning of the words. Mary, in particular, knew from Gabriel that her Son would one day lead His people, but the way in which He would lead them was still a mystery which God and time would clarify for her. So His mother remembered and pondered the words of her Son all the way back to Nazareth and for many years after that.

Our Lord having told His truth went home with them, back to the quiet and unquestioned obedience of Nazareth. There, until His public life began at about the age of thirty, the Gospels draw a curtain over His life. But we may be sure it was composed of prayer, study and deep thinking. It is from such simple things that men grow in wisdom before men.

Growing in grace before God is a deeper thing. Here, as St. Thomas Aquinas said at the end of his life, all learning is like straw compared with union with God and correspondence with His graces. Christ, being God's Son, was in perfect union with Him. All the graces that human beings need were Christ's in perfect abundance befitting the king of all saints.

Before God and men these last years were radiantly calm. The struggles of Christ's public ministry were far away; the cross cast only a small shadow. How joyously beautiful was Nazareth in those years only Mary knew completely.

O Mary, Mother of Jesus, teach us to seek God in all our sorrows and joys. Help us to find Him, and in the silence of communion with Him to listen to the wisdom of His answers. Above all, help us to learn that we too must love the house of our Father and do His work of worship and salvation. Help us to be His witness, bringing His light to all the dark corners of our neighborhood and the whole world, now and at the hour of our death.

Part Three

THE

SORROWFUL

MYSTERIES

X INTRODUCTION TO

THE SORROWFUL MYSTERIES

THE joyful mysteries close with the enigmatic statement that Jesus returned to Nazareth and "grew in grace and wisdom before God and men." Between the time of this statement and the emergence of Jesus at the beginning of His public ministry, almost twenty years elapsed.

The New Testament is silent about those years, but from the obvious power with which Jesus appeared on the public scene we are sure He had in that silent time perfected Himself in all the exceptional qualities of human wisdom, self-discipline and grave or smiling mannerliness that endeared Him to everyone and which were quite at variance with His birth in a stable or His life as a small-town boy working at the carpenter's trade.

In the full strength of His manhood, then, Jesus comes out of silence to tell men the story of God's mercy and the new law of love that jumps every barrier of narrowness or intolerance.

There is a picture of Our Lord's baptism in the Jordan, painted by El Greco, which is for me the most satisfactory picture of Jesus I have ever seen. Our Lord is kneeling on one knee on a waterworn boulder at the edge of the Jordan. John the Baptist, lean and attenuated from much penance, and clad in a brief garment of camel's hair, stands slightly above Our Saviour, pouring water from a shell in two fine trickles over His head.

Jesus is shown in the full strength of disciplined and muscular manhood. His long hands are folded in prayer, His neck is slightly inclined. His Nazarite beard and hair make a fine frame for the gentle face, which is serenely beautiful and intelligent without sacrifice of any of the qualities we usually associate with manliness.

This strong, masculine representation makes it possible for us to envisage Jesus walking the countryside, working at the nets, and sleeping out under the stars. It also enables us to see Jesus clearly in every vigorous act of His public ministry: teaching, working stupendous miracles, driving the money-changers from the temple, weeping over Jerusalem, writing in the dust in defense of the repentant Magdalene. Such a man has the physical presence that goes with kingship, and the wild triumph of Palm Sunday; such a man adds to the depth of tragedy we experience in meditating on the sorrowful mysteries.

Each set of mysteries has its own atmosphere. The joyful mysteries are filled with sunshine and childlike joy. The atmosphere of the sorrowful mysteries is murky with night, charged with horror, weakness, and ingratitude. From the agony in the garden to the agony of the crucifixion we behold a strong and perfect man, who was also God, derided, shamed and brutalized by every torture the warped brains of his tormentors could devise. It is an obscene thing to witness the suffering of any human being, however mean, however shameful the character of his manhood; but a new depth of horror is reached when the suffering one is innocent, good, kind, beautiful—and God.

Seeing Our Lord as El Greco saw Him helps to see Jesus as Mary saw Him during the hours of His passion. Jesus was her only Child. She knew Him with a mother's fondness, in which His manly grace and mental qualities were magnified. That Mary also knew Jesus as God's Son, amply shown at the marriage feast in Cana, lifted her love to adoration. The agony of seeing Jesus tortured was in Mary's case almost past imagination.

We may be sure that the apostles and disciples who witnessed each step of the tragedy carried every scrap of news to Jesus' Mother. We may be sure Mary anguished in unity with Jesus in every step of His passion and death. The evangelists are silent about what Mary experienced. The only reference to the Mother of Jesus is found in St. John. "Now there stood by the cross of Jesus His mother and His mother's sister, Mary of Clopas, and Mary Magdalene. When Jesus therefore saw His mother and the disciple standing by, whom He loved, He saith to His mother, 'Woman, behold thy Son.'

"Then He saith to the disciple, 'Behold thy mother.'

"And from that hour the disciple took her to his own." JOHN XIX, 25-27.

Did Mary know *why* Jesus had to die? It must have been so, and it explains much of the reticence of the sacred writers. Our Lady was so perfectly in accord with God's will that the sacrifice of the cross and the suffering preceding it would have been accepted by her with dignity and love. Her role was in keeping with her eminence and vision. The sorrow she felt was a mother's sorrow that her Son, so good, beautiful and kind, should be shamefully battered into the mere semblance of a man before the very crowds that had shouted *hosanna* to His name.

The sorrowful mysteries are Mary's sorrows in union with her Son. Against the background of this tragic understanding all the scenes of the passion can be observed in proper perspective.

The sorrowful mysteries are also soul-searching meditations on the horror of sin and the rebellion of the will against God. In Gethsemane, Jesus shuddered at the horror and *sweated* blood. During His brutal scourging Our Lord *shed* blood for all the indulgences of the flesh: unlawful sexual pleasure, gluttony, drunkenness, luxury. He was scourged for our offenses.

In the crowning with thorns He suffered for the sins of the mind: pride, envy, malice, desire—the list is endless.

In carrying His cross Jesus atoned for all the evil journeys of men since time began: to unlawful trysts in miserly pursuit of money, to robbery, violence, murder, or the insane search for amusement at any cost.

Last of all, on the cross He redeemed us from original sin and opened for us the gates of the new spiritual paradise.

Sorrow and sin, sin and sorrow! We can learn the full, dreadful meaning of these words in meditating on the passion of Our Lord.

THE FIRST

SORROWFUL MYSTERY

The Agony in the Garden

"This is your hour, and the power of darkness."

THESE are the stark words addressed by Jesus to the chief priests and the temple officers who had come to arrest Him in the garden of Gethsemane. Ronald Knox in his edition of the New Testament translates the phrases in a slightly different way: "But your time has come now, and darkness has its will."

These words of Jesus accurately set the mood of the scene in the garden of olives. It is the garden of Eden in reverse: Eden was the earthly paradise, sunny, luxurious in its profusion of fruit and flowers, serene under the benign rule of God. In Gethsemane, gloom and shade are everywhere under the twisted trees, with their oily, bitter fruit, as if this were the garden of the prince of darkness. Before we walk into its shadows it is well that we should recall what has gone before.

The public ministry had come to a close with its unbelievable miracles, the raising of Lazarus and the feeding of the five thousand in the desert. The triumph of Palm Sunday was the crown of all the works preceding it—the popular demonstration in favor of a leader with miraculous gifts, capable of restoring the kingship and the ancient power of Israel.

The Pharisees, high priests and temple officers wanted none of this. The Pharisees hated Jesus because He preached a spiritual kingdom at variance with their vested interests; the high priests and temple officers were content with things the way they were. Tools of Rome, with fat salaries and many perquisites, they quivered with each denunciation by Jesus, who called them "whited sepulchers." They were determined to seize Him at the first opportunity.

They needed a traitor, one with the inside information on the movements of Jesus, so that they could take Him at some secret time and place when the multitudes would not rush to His defense. There was no necessity to search for their man. He presented himself—the apostle, Judas Iscariot.

St. John says with no mincing of words, Judas "was a thief, and having the purse, used to take what was put therein." As the treasurer of the apostles, Judas had apparently looked forward to an opulent future in which Jesus would be a great king with money flowing into his treasury from all the kingdoms of the world. When it became increasingly clear to Judas that the kingdom was to be a spiritual one, in which poverty was one of the chief virtues, he saw all his golden plans nullified.

In that moment of revulsion he went to the priests with an offer to deliver Jesus into their hands—for a price. A deal was made. For thirty pieces of silver, Judas agreed to betray his Master. It was enough to buy a field.

It may be well to say of Judas, at this point, that he perhaps didn't think Christ would be put to death. Imprisoned, yes, taken out of circulation for a time until the multitudes could forget Him and His strange notions. Only in the light of such a surmise is it possible to understand the cry of Judas, "I have sinned in betraying innocent blood," after the sentence of death had been passed upon Our Lord by the Sanhedrin.

With festering treason in his heart, Judas sat down to the Paschal supper with Jesus and the disciples. Our Lord was oppressed by the thought of Judas' treason. With a sigh He announced that one of those at table would betray Him. The announcement caused complete consternation. In the midst of the hubbub of denial Peter asked John, who reclined next to Our Lord at table, to ask the traitor's name of Jesus.

Then, as St. John tells the story, Jesus answered, " 'He it is, for whom I shall dip this morsel and give it to him.'

"Dipping therefore the morsel, He taketh and giveth it to Judas, the son of Simon Iscariot. And after the morsel, then did Satan enter into him. Jesus therefore saith to him, 'That which thou dost, do quickly.'

"But no one at the table understood why he said this to him; for some thought, since Judas had the purse, that Jesus was saying to him, 'Buy what things we need for the feast' or that he should give something to the poor. He therefore, having received the morsel, straightway went out; and it was night." JOHN XIII, 26-30.

"It was night." There is a chill in the words that caused the poet in St. Augustine to cry out, "Darkness went out to darkness." From the Light of the World Judas scurried away to the prince of darkness—into the night, forever.

It was night when Jesus and the disciples, after the beautiful sermon, which Judas didn't hear, walked out of the city across the span arching the brook of Cedron. St. Mark implies that while they were walking toward Gethsemane, Jesus said, " 'All ye shall be scandalized, for it is written, "I will smite the shepherd, and the sheep shall be dispersed," but after I am risen, I will go before you into Galilee.'

"Peter said to Him, 'Even if all shall be scandalized, yet not I.'

"And Jesus saith to him, 'Amen I say to thee, today, this very night, before the cock crow twice, thou shalt deny Me thrice.'

"But he spoke all the more vehemently, 'Though I should have to die with Thee, I will not deny Thee.'

"And in like manner said they all." MARK XIV, 27-31.

The little band entered the walled garden.

Gethsemane! The word means olive press—a name of anguish forevermore after this night. The heavy sandals of the group were muffled in the thick grass. A faint perfume of the spikenard, poured over the head of Jesus by Mary Magdalene, breathed out under the close-ranked trees mingled with the smell of the spring earth. The trees, silver on moonlight nights, seemed made of iron under the early night sky. There was a chill in the air, flowing down the hillside.

Jesus had often come here to pray, drawing aside into the shadow, while the apostles discussed the events of the day in low tones. On this night the Lord called Peter and James and John to go with Him further on into the darkness.

They heard Him making deep sighs of dismay. In the heavy dusk they could barely see the contorted blur of that beloved face. He was wringing His hands. There was anguish in His voice as He addressed them. "My soul is sorrowful unto death. Stay ye here and watch."

In their years together they had never seen Him so disturbed. One of His great qualities in their eyes was the tranquil and princely way in which He met each event of life.

"And going forward a little He fell upon the ground," St. Mark tells us, "and prayed that if it were possible the hour might pass away from Him. And he said '*Abba,* Father, all things are possible to Thee, turn aside this cup from Me; yet not what I will, but what Thou wilt.'"

St. Luke, at this point, adds a poignant note to St. Mark's account, "And there appeared to Him an angel from heaven to strengthen Him. And falling into an agony He prayed the more earnestly; and His sweat became as drops of blood falling down to the ground."

Now, as never before, He needed human comfort. Rising from His agony He came to his favorite three. They were sitting on the grass huddled in their mantles, sound asleep. He said to Peter, " 'Simon, sleepest thou? Couldst thou not watch one hour? Watch ye and pray, lest ye enter into temptation. The spirit indeed is willing, but the flesh is weak.'

"And again He departed and prayed, saying the same words. And again He came and found them asleep, for their eyes were heavy; and they knew not what to answer Him. And He cometh the third time, and saith to them, 'Sleep on now, and rest! Enough! The hour is come; behold, the Son of Man is to be betrayed into the hands of sinners. Arise, let us go; behold, he that betrayeth me is at hand.'

"And straightway, whilst he was yet speaking, cometh Judas, one of the Twelve, and with him a multitude with swords and clubs, from the high priests and the scribes and the elders. Now he that betrayed Him had given them a sign, saying, 'Whomsoever I shall kiss, that is He; seize Him and lead Him away carefully.'

"And when he was come, straightway he went up to Him and saith, 'Rabbi!' And he kissed Him.

"And they laid hands on Him and seized Him. But one of the bystanders, drawing his sword, struck the servant of the high priest and cut off his ear. And Jesus answering said to them: 'Are ye come out, as against a robber, with swords and clubs to arrest Me? Day after day I was with you in the temple teaching, and ye seized Me not. But that the scriptures may be fulfilled.'

"And all left Him and fled." MARK XIV, 37-50.

The Agony in the Garden is a deeply moving, deeply human mystery. It is deeply human in that Our Lord for the one time in His recorded life anguished over the impending torment of His suffering and death.

To understand His anguish we must remember that Jesus was in the full flower of His vigorous manhood. Suddenly He saw the full, terrible ordeal in which His very strength would insure that He felt every massive and exquisite twinge of pain. The weak faint and find surcease; the strong know pain until the last moment of death.

Over and above Our Lord's strength was His human intelligence, which we can see from all His words and actions was of the highest order: quick in perception, brilliant in formulation, far-ranging in its scope. Added to this was His brilliant imagination, so adept in selecting for Himself and His auditors the pictures that made His parables and comparisons at once memorable and poetically beautiful.

The strong but stolid man often seems exceptionally brave. His quickness in action arises from the fact that he is geared to act without seeing what the consequences are, or what will follow from any given set of circumstances. Danger has little meaning for him. But the strong man gifted with the highest qualities of intellect and imagination trembles before danger and death. Yet his courage is of the highest order, since he must outface what he sees and, despite the horror he so clearly comprehends, must follow the course set for him.

Last but not least was Our Lord's complete understanding of why the sacrifice was necessary. That is, sin original and sin actual: the sin of Adam and Eve, and the sins of all men, their murders, lusts, cruelties, pride and thefts "to the last syllable of recorded time." It was the upper and nether millstones of sin that crushed Jesus to the ground. Both as man and God He could see into the full horror of the human will's rebellion and apostasy. Judas, the sleeping apostles, the triple denial of Peter later in that same night—all spotlight the horror that bathed Our Lord in a bloody sweat at what He saw and what He knew.

The night, the shuddering terror of suffering and death, the bloody sweat of revulsion, the treason of His special friends, asleep when they might have comforted Him, are capped in the end with the kiss of a traitor.

How heroically Jesus outfaced terror in the garden is revealed by His stern confrontation of Judas and his cohorts. The irony of His question to Judas, "Thou betrayest the son of man with a kiss?" reported by St. Luke, is deepened in St. Matthew with, "Friend, for what a purpose art thou come?"

The oblique but none the less terrible rebuke to Judas is followed by Our Lord's grave reproach to the temple police and their officers. "Are ye come out as against a robber with swords and clubs? When I was daily with you in the temple ye stretched not forth your hands against Me. *But* this is your hour, and the power of darkness."

According to St. John, it was Peter, so soon to deny Christ, who drew a sword when they came to seize Jesus and cut off the ear of Malchus, the high priest's servant.

But Jesus commanded Peter to put up his sword, saying that the scriptures must be fulfilled. Then having asked that His apostles be not harmed He held out His hands to be bound. Like a lamb led to the slaughter He left the garden, and the disciples fled.

O Holy Mother, through the agony of your Son in Gethsemane, teach us to see the horror of sin, treason and disloyalty. Teach us to avoid evil, cruelty and hatred. Help us to stay alert in the presence of Jesus; help us to pray against temptation, now and at the hour of our death.

THE SECOND

SORROWFUL MYSTERY

The Scourging at the Pillar

JESUS came to His scourging after an interrogation continued all night and far into the morning. His ordeal shows familiar and startling similarity to modern, police-state interrogation, and in the trial of Jesus there are other striking parallels with modern times in which mobs are played upon and wrought up to frenzy for the purpose of achieving political objectives.

St. John tells us Jesus was first brought before the high priest Annas. This enormously rich and oily old man manipulated and dominated the high priesthood for decades through the election of his five sons to that office. Annas' son-in-law Caiaphas was the high priest of the year on the night when Jesus was taken before the hastily assembled Sanhedrin.

St. John's narrative has caused some confusion among commentators because he calls both Annas and Caiaphas high priest. It may be conjectured that this is much the same formality we employ when speaking of ex-presidents of the United States as presidents. Annas had been high priest from A.D. 6–15 and probably still retained the courtesy title in the eyes of St. John when he came to write his Gospel.

Annas was undoubtedly the power behind the throne. When Jesus was brought into the luxurious palace of Annas, we may be sure that the arrogant old man in his silken robes, surrounded by his guards and intimates, examined Jesus with careful attention in the flickering lights, massed in stands before his divan. It would be Annas' estimate of the man that would guide the strategy to be followed in securing the condemnation of Our Lord and its confirmation by Pontius Pilate.

What did Annas discover? By hinting that Jesus was a secret conspirator and asking Him to state His doctrine, Annas evoked from Our Lord a stinging rebuke that His doctrine had been openly preached. If Annas wanted to hear what the doctrine was, he could ask those who had heard Jesus in the temple and elsewhere.

For this reply Jesus was slapped across the mouth by one of the bystanders. He endured the blow with perfect dignity, asking why He was struck for telling the truth.

What Annas discovered in this encounter is easy to see. First he saw a kingly person with a sharp mind, who refused to be intimidated where truth was concerned. Jesus knew, as well as Annas, that the secret temple police had recorded all His statements as they were made about the country. To be led astray by the naïve trickery of Annas would have been to give countenance to untruth.

This revelation gave Annas the basis of his plan for speedy condemnation. Let there be no fumbling. Get false witnesses to confuse truth that could be used to inflame the mob. Then go to the heart of the matter and let Jesus declare *who* He was.

So it happened. From the quarters of Annas, Jesus was led across the palace courtyard to the equally luxurious house of Caiaphas, where a quorum of the Sanhedrin had been hastily and unlawfully assembled, since it was forbidden to try cases at night.

Not everything about Our Lord's trial is set down in the Scriptures. There would probably have been ample time for Annas to send his son-in-law a message briefing him on the procedure to be followed.

Once again, with His hands bound like a criminal, Jesus faced an assemblage of outwardly dignified old men sitting in a semicircle, this time with Caiaphas as president enthroned in the center. Caiaphas wasted no time. First, with cynical legality, he called up his false witnesses, probably from the secret temple police. Their chief contribution was that Jesus had threatened to destroy the temple and rebuild it in three days. Jesus had on this occasion been speaking of the temple of His body and its resurrection, as St. John tells us.

Our Lord ignored the perjured hirelings, but the damage had been done. That Jesus had been *accused* of threatening to destroy the temple was enough.

Very likely, once the accusation was on record the secret police began to circulate the rumor in the bazaars and places of assembly.

Pious Jews loved the temple, not merely because of its magnificence, which made it one of the wonders of the world, but because it was God's house, holy beyond measure. That anyone should threaten to destroy God's house put him beyond the pale of mercy. He was in mob-eyes worthy of death.

Then Caiaphas moved swiftly to the denouement. With great drama he asked Jesus, "I adjure Thee by the living God to tell us whether thou art the Christ, the Son of God."

The echoes of the high priest's voice died against the gilded ceiling. Light played on the wrinkled faces leaning to catch Our Lord's reply.

"I am."

It was an unequivocal answer in which Jesus declared Himself equal with God, all the more astounding because He added, "Hereafter 'ye shall see the Son of Man seated on the right of the Power and coming upon the clouds of heaven.' " Christ had claimed both the rule and judgment of His people.

In the midst of the outcries we can see the hands of Caiaphas rending his silken tunic as he screams, "He hath blasphemed! What further need have we of witnesses?" And they answered, "He is worthy of death."

Then the rage and hatred in their hearts put aside all pretense of law, justice and dignity. Jesus was blindfolded, and the raging old men cuffed Him and punched Him, pulled His beard, covered His face with their spittle. They were all jeering and crying, "Prophesy to us, O Christ, who was it that struck thee?"

Jesus never uttered a cry.

How long the abuse continued we do not know. But in going out of the council chamber, Our Lord was led through the courtyard and looked on the prince of the apostles who had thrice denied Him. One reproachful look was enough for Peter. Rushing from the courtyard, he walked the empty streets sobbing his repentance.

Very probably Jesus was confined in some cubbyhole or secret cell for the remainder of the night. We may be sure, from what we have seen, that He was *brutally* confined, in the best tradition of modern jailors.

It is likely that the Sanhedrin reconvened very early to make their con-

demnation legal with the first light. What the leaders had planned was carefully designed to put increasing pressure on Pontius Pilate—a weak, stubborn
and sometimes brutal man. Pilate alone could order the actual execution, but
on two previous occasions Pilate had been in trouble with the dreaded Emperor Tiberius. This knowledge was Annas' trick card.

The weary Saviour, after His formal condemnation, was led bound to
the palace-fortress of Antonia. Its great squat tower dominated the temple-
area like the monolithic power of Rome.

Whatever Pilate may have been, he was no fool. Clad in vivid scarlet
and sitting on his curule chair in the superb courtyard of the castle, Pilate
examined Jesus with the sharp eyes of a trained soldier, and what he saw
obviously impressed him.

The Jews, because of the danger of incurring ritual impurity, could not
enter the great courtyard of the fortress. They probably jammed themselves
into the covered entryway, and crowded the streets outside.

What took place in the ensuing trial is as modern as today's newspaper.
Jesus was presented to Pilate as a seditious man, stirring up the people and
refusing to pay tribute to Caesar. Here again a half-truth was used as an
instrument. When Pilate carefully questioned Our Lord the Procurator was
convinced that the kingdom of Jesus was spiritual, "not of this world," as
Our Lord claimed.

At this point, since he had convinced himself that no sedition was involved, Pilate should have set Jesus free. Instead, he told the Jewish leaders
of his findings. They insisted that Jesus was stirring up the people all over
the country.

Then the weak but stubborn Pilate saw a way out of his dilemma. King
Herod Antipas had come up for the feast and was in residence in the Has-
monean Palace a short distance away. Because he knew that Our Lord was a
Galilean, Pilate sent Him before the Tetrarch.

Pilate no doubt considered this a clever move. He and the king had not
been friends for a long time. Herod's judgment would either strengthen
Pilate's hand in dealing with the mob and their leaders or, if the judgment
proved to be against Jesus, would remove much of the blame for sending
Our Lord to the cross.

The interview between Jesus and the murderer of John the Baptist was filled with drama. Jesus stood before the jewelled court. He was known as a wonder-worker, and they all hoped for a sign, something that would amuse them in an idle hour. So Herod greeted Jesus with kindly expectancy and asked Him questions. Our Lord answered not a word. His scorn withered them to an uneasy silence.

Then the leaders of the people broke into a volley of accusations, vehemently repeating all the half-truths they had told Pilate, along with the accusation of blasphemy, which Herod as a Jew could be expected to understand.

Still Jesus said nothing. A movement went through the assemblage; they tittered and whispered and began to jeer at Jesus as a king without power. They threatened Him with their swords, daring Him to give a sign, like village atheists daring God to strike them dead.

But the sign was not given. The silence oppressed them at length, and in mockery of Jesus' kingship they brought out a bright robe such as kings wear, draped it about him and then paraded Jesus back to Pilate.

The mocking gesture was not lost on Pilate. But he must have admitted to himself that Jesus did look like a king, now more than ever, so he made one more attempt to save the prisoner. It had become a custom in Jerusalem to release a prisoner before the feast of the Pasch. The accusations against Jesus seemed to Pilate compounded of envy and the spite of the Jewish leaders. Perhaps if he gave them a choice between a known and hardened criminal and this kingly person, he would be able to sway the mob to his side.

There had been a recent riot in the city. Its leader Barabbas had caused sedition and bloodshed—Jewish blood. Surely no one would choose to free this dangerous man.

Pilate faced the leaders of the muttering mob, now swollen with new arrivals. They fell silent while he gave them their choice. Christ or Barabbas?

A swelling roar was the answer, "Barabbas! Barabbas!" It was a steady, triumphant chant. The manipulators of the mob had done their work well against the blasphemer who had threatened to destroy the holy temple.

"And what shall I do with Jesus of Nazareth?" Pilate asked. The reply astounded him.

The sea of heads was stirred by a wave of hatred; the faces were contorted with rage. The roar became a scream now.

"Crucify Him! Crucify Him!" It went on and on, until Pilate made an impatient sign for silence.

Pilate drew himself up red-faced with anger, and when he spoke it was in his coldest official voice: "I have found naught in Him deserving of death . . . when I have chastised Him I will release Him!"

Turning abruptly, Pilate gave his commands for the scourging of Jesus and stalked into his own quarters.

Looking back over the foregoing events, we can see exactly the state of Our Lord when He came to His scourging. For an entire day He had been on His feet, probably without food or drink. He had been betrayed, denied, mocked, spit upon, cuffed, kicked and vilified.

The soldiers roughly took off Our Lord's garments, giving them into the hands of an officer for safekeeping. When Jesus was naked, they lashed Him securely over a low pillar.

Normally, scourging took place in the presence of lictors who counted the thirty-nine strokes as they were given. Here in Jerusalem there were no lictors, and the scourging was in the hands of brutal soldiers, recruited from the dregs of the empire. They loved savage spectacles; they also disliked Jews because of the constant trouble they caused. Now they had one in their power who professed to be the King of the Jews.

We do not know what type of scourges the soldiers used on Jesus. Was it whips that cut the flesh to ribbons? Was it chains with lead balls or bone tips that cut and bruised the flesh at the same time? The evangelists are silent on this point. They report the scourging in brief phrases that reveal the heart's protest against this indignity inflicted on Jesus, Who was so tender-hearted and compassionate with all who suffered.

The dreadful work began. A brawny arm was lifted. The scourge whistled through the air and fell, ripping into the muscular back, hips and legs. The cuts and bruises crisscrossed. Blood was spattered on the pavement in a widening circle. The scourges rose and fell.

It must have amazed them, in their brutal work, to realize at last that no cry had been uttered, no groan had escaped. What sort of man was this who infuriated them with his silent endurance? They untied His hands and His feet, bathed in blood, and repeatedly they jerked Him cruelly to a standing position.

O Holy Mother, in this dreadful scourging of your strong and beautiful Son teach us to see the horror of all those sins of the flesh for which Jesus suffered. Help us to hate cruelty; help us to hate sin—our sins—that scarred His back with scourges; help us to atone, now and at the hour of our death.

THE THIRD

SORROWFUL MYSTERY

The Crowning with Thorns

THE soldiers, jesting and laughing, pushed Jesus around among them. One of them had an idea. What a comical king of the Jews He would make! One of the men ran to get an old scarlet cloak that someone had discarded. They draped it roughly about his bleeding body.

A crown, a king must have a crown! They looked about them. Two of them snatched several strands of the thorn bush, lying there on the pavement in bundles as kindling for the fires. The thorns were sharp and long. Carefully they plaited the dried branches, shouting curses each time a thorn point pricked their fingers.

At last it was done. They pressed the crown down on the half-bent head, and trickles of blood began to course down Jesus' face. Then rudely seating Him on a high stool, they roared with merriment. What a king of the Jews!

Among the kindling was a long, dried yellow reed. His golden scepter! They stuffed it between His bound hands.

A king must receive the obedience of his subjects. The line formed as they had seen it in the past in Rome and Alexandria. Each soldier in mock adoration bent the knee. Then, as he rose, snatched the heavy reedy scepter and struck it down on top of the crown. That really made the blood flow. Some added a slap on His face for good measure.

Pilate unexpectedly appeared, and the soldiers fell silent as the Procurator looked at their handiwork. Pilate was amazed. Many strong men had died of the scourges. Jesus sat there still erect in blood-soaked majesty, a noble but pitiable figure. Surely if the crowd could see Him their lust for blood would be sated.

Commands were given. Two of the soldiers caught Jesus by the elbows and forced Him to His feet. Pilate was already walking up the staircase leading to his private quarters, and the soldiers hurried Jesus after him. At the top of the staircase was a platform from which the entire threatening mob could see the portly form of Rome's representative. Pilate was speaking, "Behold I bring Him forth to you, that ye may know I find no crime in Him."

Suddenly the mob saw between two muscular soldiers the form of their enemy, standing beside Pilate. Jesus was draped in a robe of royal scarlet, crowned with thorns, streaming with blood so that His face was crimson as the robe he wore. Dramatically Pilate intoned, "Behold the man."

The secret police and government spies had done their work well with the mob. The hissing passed from mouth to mouth. "The temple destroyer, the blasphemer even now with these Roman buffoons making a mockery of Solomon and David and their kingly past." They shouted over and over with one voice a single word: "Crucify, Crucify, Crucify!"

Pilate said to them at last, "Take Him yourselves and crucify Him; for I find no crime in Him." But the leaders stood out at the front of the mob. One of them spoke out, "We have a law, and according to the law He must die because He hath made Himself Son of God."

The term shocked Pilate. The Son of God! He fingered his golden belt and his fingers found the note his wife had sent him earlier in the day, "Have nothing to do with the blood of this just man."

From the first glance Pilate had seen there was something exceptional about Jesus—a kingliness unmistakable in word, form and action. Even after the scourging something regal still showed. And His kingdom was not of this world.

What if it were true? What if He were the son of some god? Moved with this notion, Pilate confronted Jesus where He stood in the vestibule to the Roman's private quarters. "Whence art thou?" he asked.

The weary, half-opened eyes looked at Pilate during a long silence. There was a hint of fury in Pilate's voice when he spoke to the quiet figure. "Speakest Thou not to me? Knowest Thou not that I have power to release Thee and that I have power to crucify Thee?"

The head was lifted straight. The dark eyes opened and there was a strange fire in them. "Thou would'st have no power over Me were it not given thee from above; for this cause he that hath delivered Me to thee hath the greater sin."

Pilate went out to argue with the Jewish leaders, standing in a knot at the front of the muttering crowd. To every appeal he made they returned the same answer, "He is worthy of death—crucify Him. He has blasphemed."

Finally the crowd joined the debate. "You are no friend of Caesar's. He has made Himself a king and has set Himself against Caesar." They repeated the accusation, over and over.

The argument made Pilate uneasy. Not to be the friend of Caesar was to enter a desolate climate of banishment or death. His flesh shivered at the notion. The high priests were enormously wealthy and powerful, he knew from experience. They had twice denounced him in Rome and made it stick. If they inflamed the stubborn mob against him, as they had before, there would be bloodshed and rioting, and he would be no friend of Caesar's.

With a weary shrug Pilate gave the necessary orders to a Centurion. He walked back across the courtyard and mounted the low steps of the judgment seat. Across the wide courtyard the crowd growled and muttered like an angry dog. Jesus and Barabbas were brought out below the platform.

A sudden fury boiled in Pilate's mind. They had beaten him, but at least he would have the last word.

He spoke a word to a soldier. A golden basin was brought and a crystal pitcher. Standing before his ivory chair, Pilate slowly washed his hands and dried them on a purple-edged napkin. In a loud voice he cried out that all might hear. "I am innocent of this blood; do ye look to it."

The Procurator sat down heavily in the chair. First he commanded that Barabbas be released and watched the frenzy of the crowd as they welcomed him. Then turning his glance to Jesus he said the fateful words of the Roman sentence: "Go to the cross!"

In the crowning with thorns we have a tragic commentary on all the innocent of the world who have fallen into the hands of ignorant and heartless executioners. It was the soldiers' privilege to do with Jesus anything their sadistic minds could suggest.

Even after the brutal lashing He seemed unbroken. The crowning with thorns and the clownish homage testified to that fact, and to their wish to see Him humiliated, begging for mercy. But He uttered not a sound.

How our loud pride is rebuked, our fury against those we envy or hate, the thronging evil desires we are never able to compass. For these sins of *theirs* and *ours* He suffered his divine head to be crowned, He endured mockery and derision.

O Holy Mother, teach us not to hate. Deliver us from cruelty, pride and evil, and the lusts of the mind. Help us to be humble, now and at the hour of our death.

THE FOURTH

SORROWFUL MYSTERY

The Carrying of the Cross

THE last preparations were made inside the fortress. The soldiers took Jesus aside. They wrenched the scarlet cloak from His bloody back and shoulders and with fumbling fingers dressed Him again in His own clothes. There was a ringing clatter as other soldiers threw down on the stones the crossbeams of three crosses. The soldiers made jokes about the throne Jesus would so soon occupy.

A file of soldiers formed under the command of a Centurion who inspected his bronzed hundred with a baleful eye. Making their way through the busiest part of the city with three criminals was going to be an ordeal. In those winding, narrow streets anything could happen. The very stones were tainted with the blood of past riots.

The procession began to take shape at last. The two thieves, with the eight soldiers delegated to crucify them, were followed by Jesus, with the four soldiers who would nail Him to the cross.

They had been held up for a moment while the Jewish leaders argued about the placard for Jesus' cross. It said, "Jesus of Nazareth King of the Jews," in Greek, Latin and Hebrew. But the leaders had protested. "It *should* read, 'He *said* He was King of the Jews,' " they complained.

Pilate turned on them. "What is written is written," he said scornfully, and strode away to his private apartments.

The placard was hung about the neck of Jesus. The crossbeam was hoisted to His painful shoulders.

The Centurion mounted his horse. Fifty of his men followed him. Then came the poles of the three crosses, carried by brawny soldiers. The thieves were next, dragging their heavy beams, and after them Jesus, staggering a little with pain and exhaustion. Behind the prisoners the remainder of the soldiers brought up the rear of the procession.

The first part of the crowd outside the massive fortress greeted the Centurion, soldiers and thieves with hate-filled silence. But when the figure of Jesus emerged there was a howl of blended rage and triumph. They spat at Him, called Him foul and filthy names, loaded Him with curses. Fists were shaken. Fingers made gestures of derision. Several times when the crowd pressed in too closely the Centurion turned with a scowl of rebuke and warning.

Did Mary stand there in the narrow street watching her Son go by? Tradition says she did, and there is nothing that would seem to rule out Our Lady's presence.

Though she had steeled her heart, we can imagine the anguish she endured in seeing her Child so horribly disfigured. He had been her beautiful baby; He had been so wonderful in His manhood's fulfillment. And there was no chance to help Him. All she could do was cling to the strong arm of St. John, and bear the sword of sorrow piercing her heart.

Tradition tells us too that Jesus fell several times on the journey to Calvary. Weakened from His long trial and the horrible shock and blood-letting of the scourging, it is not astonishing that Our Saviour should have fallen to the stones. It was probably after one of these falls that the Centurion began to doubt he would ever get Jesus to the cross. Something had to be done. An order had been given to crucify this man, and crucify Him he would.

Looking about him in the close-packed throng, the Centurion, from his point of vantage on the horse, saw a brawny workman. It was Simon of Cyrene trying to make his way into the city. The Centurion called to him and ordered Simon to carry the crossbeam of Jesus' cross. Simon, probably with some protest and confusion, accepted the heavy burden and joined the procession moving toward the Ephraem Gate.

Simon had no idea of the honor that was his, or the grace that awaited him. Tradition assures us that his kindness, even if it was under protest, led to the ultimate conversion of Simon and his family. It is the first miracle from the wood of the cross.

The figure of Jesus stumbled on through the hate-filled streets. He seemed lost in Himself, only half-conscious of the realities about Him. Then His head was raised at the sound of weeping. His blood-matted eyelids lifted. There, within hands-reach of Him, stood a knot of sorrowing women, lamenting His pain.

Half erect now, Jesus spoke to the little group in labored words: "Daughters of Jerusalem, weep not over Me; but weep over yourselves and over your children."

Jesus raised his head still more, and a fire of prophecy glowed in His battered face as He continued, "For behold days are coming wherein they shall say 'Blessed the barren, and the wombs that have not borne, and the breasts that have not suckled!' Then shall they begin to say to the mountains, 'Fall upon us,' and to the hills, 'Bury us'; for if in the green wood they do these things, what is to befall in the dry?"

The words with their overtones of woe caused the women to weep harder. "The green wood and the dry"—there was mystery in them.

How could they know that He was the green tree, once so beautiful with its burden of shade and flowers? How could they know that Jerusalem and its people were the dry wood? If God's justice had to be satisfied in the death of the innocent, what would happen when God's justice hunted down the sinful and the evil? The brutality wrought on Him would be multiplied a thousand times in the destruction of Jerusalem.

Jesus could see it, the coming ruin of the city, the battering engines of war, the fire and famine, the children wasting away, the slaughter and suffering, and the great golden house of God—ravaged, looted and desolate.

Outside the towering walls the procession went. The crowd poured through after it, talking and laughing with holiday triumph.

To the left went the straight line of the great road to Jaffa. All about were the green fields. The trees were in bloom.

Scanning the fields, the Centurion spotted the ideal place for the crosses. It was a little hill green with grass and trees, odd-shaped. With its two staring dots of gouged-out limestone it resembled a skull. This hill could be seen by all those moving along the Jaffa road. They would carry away from the horrid sight a healthy respect for the law and power of Rome.

Barking an order to his men, the Centurion pointed with his sword. The procession turned off from the road, along a stony path, through a small garden in which there was an unused tomb cut out of the rocks.

At the top of the hill the soldiers threw down the center poles of the crosses with cursing relief. Short shovels appeared. The men took turns, digging feverishly. Then the heavy poles were placed firmly in the pits, the earth was thrown in, and tramped down by heavy sandals. Each of the poles had a little seat jutting out from its center.

By this time the hill was dotted with people all the way to the top on every side. They laughed and pointed, looking forward to the part of the spectacle still to come.

The crossbeam was straightened out on the grass. One of the four soldiers guarding Jesus slipped the sign from the neck of his prisoner and fixed it near the top of the center pole. "Jesus of Nazareth King of the Jews," the crowd hooted.

The four soldiers began to strip Jesus of His blood-soaked clothes. When He was naked, they pushed Him down on the grass and stretched out His arms on the crossbeam. Two of them, with hammers and nails, drove spikes through the cartilage and bones of the wrists, priding themselves on their ability to miss the vital artery.

Then, two of them holding the crossbeam, two holding the feet, they carried Him to the center pole of His cross. His back was fitted above the jutting wooden seat and held there while two soldiers nailed the crossbeam to the center pole.

The crowd screamed as they watched the final strokes that drove a nail through each of the feet.

They stood back, then, and contemplated their handiwork. In the pitiless sunlight the three crosses stood, not high above the ground, so that a man might walk up and look almost at eye-level on the agonies of the crucified.

The way of the cross was the way of mercy in which Jesus atoned for all our journeys of sin, pleasure and violence. *We* stood in the teeming crowd and watched Him with the hatred of God that is sin.

Even in His unbearable misery and pain Jesus spoke to the women who wept for Him. His words are a warning that God's justice, which awaits saint and sinner, will come to every man. It is by goodness alone that we, like Simon of Cyrene, can help Him to carry His cross.

O Holy Mother, teach us to fear the justice of God. Teach us to be courteous and kind in word and deed. Help us to carry our crosses without murmuring, through the sin and hate of the world. Now and at the hour of our death.

THE FIFTH

SORROWFUL MYSTERY

The Crucifixion

IT WAS shortly after noon. The three crosses on the hill of Calvary with their burdens of human misery stood out stark against the spring sky. Already it had begun to darken, as if in prelude to a great storm.

Jesus was crucified between two thieves. The final indignity! The Holy One, spotless, without sin, was held up before His world, flanked by two brutal men convicted of robbery and violence.

Some soldiers, after their work was done, stood about to keep a semblance of order. Those not assigned to this duty lounged about on the grass behind the cross, busy with their own chatter and concerns. It was all part of the business of being a soldier.

The twelve soldiers who had done the work of the crucifixion sat in a ring fingering the sandals, girdles and tunics of the crucified, which were to be divided among them. Each had his eyes fixed on certain articles which, sold in the bazaars, would provide drinking money, a few moments of pleasure or gambling.

The discussion seems to have been amiable enough about the apportionment of most of the clothes, but there was one exception—the seamless tunic of Our Lord. It was woven in one piece, a beautiful example of the weaver's art, perfect in every detail. It had more value than all the other things put together, and no one of the twelve was willing to give it up.

Someone suggested rolling dice for the garment. So, almost at the foot of the cross, the laughter of the game went on until the lucky man had won the prize.

One tradition informs us that Our Lady had woven the seamless tunic for her Son. It is easy to picture her in the quiet of Nazareth, busy at the loom, weaving her love into every perfect stitch, at the period when Jesus was making ready to begin His public ministry. Like all mothers since time began, she wanted her Child to appear with credit before the multitudes in a robe fit for a king.

There was no longer need of it on the cross. Jesus was clad in the purple of His royal blood.

At the front of the cross a space would probably have been marked, beyond which the enemies of Jesus were not allowed to venture. Into this space, doubtless through the courtesy of the Centurion, came a little band of women and St. John. Their names are dear to us from the Gospel story: Mary the Mother of Jesus, her sister Salome, Mary of Clopas and Mary Magdalene. Tradition pictures them for us with a wealth of legends and poetic ornaments. Their presence here on the hill of Calvary is like a shaft of sunlight in the darkening atmosphere and the gloom of sorrow.

They had followed Jesus everywhere, looking after His needs and those of the Apostles. Now with womanly courage they braved the fury of the people and their leaders to link themselves with Jesus in death, as they once had been one with Him in the midst of His triumphs and miracles. Their tragedy at this moment stemmed from the fact that it was not in their power to lessen His pain in any way. They could only look up at Him with sympathetic eyes, suffering every grimace of pain and agony with Him. Weeping, they stifled their laments with hands held to mouths, that their grief might not add to the pain of their dying loved one.

Chief among the Marys was the Mother of Jesus. What the others knew of Jesus was as nothing compared with the glory of Bethlehem and the long, silent, lovely years when she had doted on His beauty and sweet responsiveness. All that she remembered was like some portrait slashed, defaced and battered almost beyond recognition. Her beautiful Child, so modest, here almost naked to the world. Slow trickles of blood fell from His hands and feet. His breathing was labored—the cords in His neck were knotted. His blood-matted head was bent, and the bluish pallor of His face crisscrossed with red scars. The mystery of God's plan and the mystery of motherhood confronted each other on Calvary.

Though the enemies of Jesus were at some little distance from the cross, they were not going to be deprived of their holiday triumph. The high priests, the temple leaders, strangers from Jewish communities of the empire who had come up for the great feast, had come out with the rabble and casual passers-by as one would go to a circus. Though Pilate had mocked them in the inscription on the cross of Jesus, they were still able to demonstrate to the public and the Romans just what kind of boastful and false king this was, hated to death by leaders and mob alike.

In a few hours it would all be over, and the great feast would begin with sundown. After that they would obey the multiple holy laws in every meticulous detail, wearing their masks of propriety and dignity.

But not here. For the leaders, the threats to their authority and money-making operations were over. It had been easy to convince the people that Jesus had threatened to destroy the temple. It was easier still to encourage them to vent their spleen on the blasphemer hanging on high in His agony.

Perhaps some bolder spirits of the mob threw spears of reeds and small pebbles at the cross, howling with pleasure each time a hit was made. One man called out: "You who said you would destroy the temple and in three days raise it up again. Destroy it now—come down from the cross if thou canst."

The mob took up the cry. "Come down from the cross. Come down from the cross and we'll believe." They spat on the ground with contempt.

A sound came from the cross. It was not a groan, but like the cry a deaf mute makes trying to break the barriers of speech. Silence fell.

Then the voice of Jesus came, bell-clear: "Father, forgive them; for they know not what they do."

For them and us it came: the blindness of hate, the confusion of sin, met by forgiveness!

The thief crucified on the left heard it. Forgiveness? The credo of the weak. He cursed. "Art thou not the Christ?" he screamed, turning in anguish toward Jesus. "If thou art, show thy power—save thyself and us."

Jesus answered nothing. It was the thief on the right who spoke. Perhaps he saw where hate and violence had led him. He too had heard stories of this Jesus and His kingdom. Only a great teacher could ask God forgiveness of His enemies out of the midst of His agony.

Making a painful effort, the second thief spoke out in rebuke, "Dost thou not even fear God, seeing that thou art under the same sentence?" He struggled with the dryness in his throat and then continued. "We have come to the cross justly, for we are receiving the fitting reward of our deeds; but this man has done naught amiss."

Then he turned his drooping head, and his voice was filled with pleading and belief, "Jesus, remember me when thou comest into thy Kingdom."

The response was immediate and clear, "Amen, I say to thee, this day thou shalt be with Me in paradise."

Jesus painfully lifted his blood-clotted lashes and gazed at the scene below: the crowds, the distant road, the spring trees such as he had known in Nazareth, heavy with pink and white flowers. His eyes found the beautiful face of his mother, ravaged with tears and sorrow. Beside her was the disciple He had loved for his open heart. They would need each other now.

The voice of Jesus was full of affection as he spoke the labored words: "Woman, behold thy son."

Then he said to the beloved disciple, "Behold thy Mother."

There was solemnity in the charge. The grave form of address for his Mother indicated something more than her motherhood for John, John's sonship for her. She was the Woman promised outside the gates of paradise. In the new spiritual paradise, which the good thief had just accepted, Mary's motherhood was extended to us all. She had been the virgin instrument of salvation for all men; at the cross she became the Mother of all men by spiritual adoption. St. John himself in his gospel says, "from that hour the disciple took her to his own."

Tradition bears out the words by telling us that Mary lived with St. John until her death and assumption. She is our Mother of Sorrows, given to us from the cross, and it is through her help and intercession that we are enabled to turn sorrow into glory without end.

During the time when Jesus was giving consolation from the cross, forgiveness of His enemies, the promise of paradise to the good thief and the gift of His mother to us, the darkness on the hill was growing in intensity. No doubt the taunts and malice of Christ's enemies persisted. Yet, when they heard His messages of consolation and looked about them in the thickening darkness, some of the mob must have grown uneasy. Those with even a shred of good will or thoughtfulness must have admitted in their hearts that Jesus was dying like a king conferring final and immortal favors from his throne.

We can see it so hauntingly: the tired figure gasping for breath, almost drained of blood. In the near distance on the Jaffa road the chariots rattling by.

Then Jesus spoke once more. It was a cry that seemed torn from his dying heart, "*Eloi Eloi, lama sabachthani,* My God My God why hast Thou forsaken Me?"

Men are never so alone as in death. The word of sympathy and love does not penetrate into that loneliness, and while the body fights against extinction, the soul in terrible isolation awaits the passage to judgment.

Jesus, having taken on the form of man, wished to endure all that man endures, including the terrible loneliness of death, when all that life means is gathered in one terrible struggle, and even God seems far away. So He cried to the Father as men today cry out in their death agony, saying, "My Jesus, mercy."

We may be sure that the high priests and scribes rejoiced in thinking that the cry meant Jesus had been forsaken by God. To them it would be triumphantly clear that they had seen the shattering of His last hope.

Among the ignorant, filled with old wives' tales about the return of the prophet Elias in his fiery chariot, the words had a different meaning. So they said to each other, "He's calling Elias." Pressing as close as they dared, they watched the cross and the darkening sky, probably wondering, in some fear, if Elias would come to take Jesus down from the cross.

Actually, the words Jesus quoted are from Psalm 21, one of the great Messianic prophecies. David's words, penned some thousand years before the crucifixion, are an amazing description of it and what it will mean to the end of time:

"*. . . I am a worm and no man: the reproach of men and
the outcast of the people.
All they that saw me have laughed me to scorn: they
have spoken with the lips and wagged the head.
Many calves have surrounded me: fat bulls have besieged me
They have opened their mouths against me, as a lion
ravening and roaring.
I am poured out like water; and all my bones are
scattered.
My heart is become like wax melting in the midst
of my bowels.*

My strength is dried up like a potsherd, and my tongue
*   hath cleaved to my jaws: and thou hast brought me*
*   down into the dust of death.*
For many dogs have encompassed me: the council of the
*   malignant hath besieged me.*
They have dug my hands and feet.
They have numbered all my bones
And they have looked and stared upon me.
They have parted my garments amongst them: and
*   upon my vesture they cast lots."*

The vivid detail in the first half of the psalm almost makes us believe that David stood on Calvary watching the slow death of the world's Saviour.

Hardly remarkable is the last half, which sums up for mankind the value and effects of the sacrifice of the cross:

"All the ends of the earth shall remember, and
*   shall be converted to the Lord:*
And all the kindreds of the Gentiles shall adore in
*   his sight.*
For the kingdom is the Lord's; and he shall have
*   dominion over the nations.*
All the fat ones of the earth have eaten and have
*   adored: all they that go down to the earth shall*
*   fall before him.*
And to him my soul shall live: and my seed shall serve
*   him.*
There shall be declared to the Lord a generation to come:
*   and the heavens shall shew forth his justice to a*
*   people that shall be born, which the Lord hath made."*[1]

The sacrifice of the cross shall be carried to the ends of the earth. All peoples and races shall adore Him and be saved. The spiritual man shall be God's man, the work of the new creation.

In giving us these clues from the cross, Our Lord points out to us the necessity of constantly searching the Scriptures for the prophecies that He

---

[1] The quotation from Psalm 21 is the Douay Version.

fulfilled. We cannot have the wonderful privilege of hearing Jesus expound the psalms and prophecies as He did for Cleophas and his companion on the road to Emmaus on Easter morning, but we can read the psalms with attention and devotion, asking Jesus to speak to our hearts.

In His dying loneliness Our Lord turned to the great prayers of His people for comfort . . . pointing out to us the love we should have for the wonderful prayers of the Church in every hour of decision, joy or tragedy.

Still praying within himself, Jesus spoke again: "I thirst."

For almost twenty-four hours Jesus had been in the shadow of pain and death. There is no indication during His trial, scourging, and crucifixion that anyone offered Him anything more than bitter comfort. Thus the cry of Jesus "I thirst" comes down to us with poignant sadness.

Jesus thirsted as man. His body was almost completely dried out from the scourging and slow bleeding. Did He think back to the pure springs of Nazareth and His youth, or the cool waters along the roads beside which He and His disciples had walked? David at various places in the psalms describes the thirst of Our Lord with terrifying realism.

But Jesus also thirsted as God. From the agony of the cross, now almost finished, He thirsted for the souls of men, longed for the hearts of sinners.

The response to His cry was the response sinners too often make when Jesus opens for them the way of grace and salvation.

St. John tells us that a "bystander," one of the soldiers, perhaps, took a sponge, dipped it in vinegar, and held it up to the parched and bluish lips on a long stalk of reed.

Tasting the final bitterness, Jesus said: "It is finished."

Everything that the prophets had said of the atoning death of the Saviour had been accomplished in the most minute detail. Jesus had come into the world to die that men might be redeemed through the understanding of God's great love for the human race.

Now Jesus turned His inward gaze toward His Father. Like an obedient son He had fulfilled all the horror that He had seen in His agony in the garden. Like a tired child putting his trusting fingers into his father's hand, Our Lord said His final prayer from the cross: "Father, into Thy hands I commend My spirit."

Then crying out with a loud voice of triumph Jesus died.

Immediately, the first signs of His triumph were felt on the hill of Calvary and in the Holy City. The earth shuddered in the gloom. Crying to one another in alarm, the high priests and the leaders of the mob ran from the hill, back to the shelter of the city walls. In the half-darkness they could hear eerie voices crying from the tombs of the dead. The rainbowed veil that marked off God's house in the temple was suddenly torn from top to bottom; the foundations shook down to the mother rock.

Looking up at the cross, forsaken except for the soldiers and the friends of Jesus, the Centurion gazed long at the quiet figure there, and then exclaimed, "Truly He was the Son of God," an exclamation that will go on ringing to the end of time.

Only one thing more remained. When the fearful leaders rallied their spirits and cynically demanded that the three bodies be taken from the crosses in respect for the great holy day at hand, soldiers came and broke the legs of the two thieves to make sure they would die of shock.

It was obvious that Jesus was dead. They probably felt His legs and feet and lifted up the noble head, like a king's even in death.

Perhaps they too had heard the rumor that He would rise from the dead. Perhaps they had been expressly commanded to make doubly sure He was dead. In any event, one of the soldiers took a lance and drove it into the side of Jesus.

All standing there must have cried out in amazement, for there came forth a gush of blood and water. It was the last symbolic token of love for mankind. Out of that yearning, loving heart came the last gush of redeeming blood and the saving water which in baptism would begin creation anew.

The triumph of Jesus had begun.

O Holy Mother, keep us near the cross with you that we may never forget how great a love redeemed us. In all our sufferings and sorrows help us to see that we are one with Jesus in doing God's will—now and at the hour of our death.

Part Four

THE

GLORIOUS

MYSTERIES

XI INTRODUCTION TO
THE GLORIOUS MYSTERIES

THE glorious mysteries are refulgent with the pure light of eternity flowing down upon the world. In this radiance the triumph of Christ through time, and of all those who believe in Him, begins to take shape.

Before the resurrection, Our Lord's human appearance and personality are the dominant notes in the Gospel. After the resurrection the godhead shines through His impassible body in unmistakable fashion. He appears at will in one place or other. He walks into locked rooms without the opening of a door. The apostles are somewhat in awe of Him.

Not only in body is He changed. No longer is it necessary for Him to suggest solutions in pictures and parables. Command is in His person, voice and directions. Over and over He stresses, to the stubborn-minded among the apostles, that His kingdom is to be spiritual and spiritualized. There is no longer any reign but the spirit; there is no longer any true power but in the spirit.

For forty days after His resurrection He carefully instructs the disciples on the organization of the kingdom, and He crowns that instruction with the appointment of Peter to rule the flock of God.

Yet Jesus is always conscious of their frailty. He gives them the old familiar courtesy, love and gentleness, even to the extent of repeating the miraculous draught of fishes with which He had first impressed them long ago in their happy life together.

From a farewell feast, probably in the upper room, He walks out with them to the mountaintop, where they watch Him ascend in triumph to join His Father in the rule of the world.

We watch the apostles and the Mother of Jesus, after His going, secluded and in prayer, awaiting the fulfillment of the Holy Spirit.

Then on the mystic morning of Pentecost the Holy Spirit descends in fire. The last age of the world has dawned, in which the Third Person of the Blessed Trinity stands fully revealed to the world, consoling, inspiring and strengthening all those who work for Christ in the final battle with materialism and hatred.

It is one of the glories of the rosary that it teaches us to see in dazzling beauty the rewards that will come to us all in the resurrection of the dead after the final judgment.

One conceived without sin had no need to wait for that hour, of which no man knows. Because she was full of grace, because she fulfilled the will of God in pure perfection, because she is the Mother of God, Mary came to the rewards of her assumption and coronation immediately at the end of her life.

In her glorification Our Lord encourages us to see the glories that await us all when time is done. She brought Jesus to us; she can keep us with Him if we ask her.

THE FIRST

GLORIOUS MYSTERY

The Resurrection

"And when the sabbath was over, Mary Magdalene, and Mary the mother of James, and Salome, bought spices that they might go and anoint Him. And very early in the morning on the first day of the week they come to the tomb, the sun being now risen. And they said one to another, 'Who will roll us away the stone from the entrance of the tomb?'

"And on looking up they see that the stone hath been rolled back. For it was very great. And on entering the tomb they saw a young man seated on the right side, clad in a white robe; and they were terrified. But he saith to them, 'Be not terrified. Ye seek Jesus of Nazareth, who was crucified. He is risen, He is not here. Behold the place where they laid Him! But go, tell His disciples and Peter that He goeth before you into Galilee; there ye shall see Him, as He told you.'" MARK XVI, 1-7.

The scene is set in a garden—a garden whose center is a rock-hewn tomb. It is a borrowed tomb, in which the body of Jesus had been hurriedly buried because the great Sabbath of the Passover was at hand when all work was forbidden.

We may reconstruct that spring morning from the many mornings in spring we ourselves have experienced. The sky is flawless blue. Warmth is there, tempered with a slight breeze. From the earth comes forth the fragrance of growing things, and above all the odor of fresh-turned earth, much like the smell of bread, crusty and brown from the oven. Everything breathes of life and resurrection. The most gnarled old trees put out a few green leaves. Life surges in a thousand waves over the ancient mummy of the earth, throwing off its wrappings of winter.

We may well believe that Joseph of Arimathea's garden, near the low hill of Calvary, was beautiful on the long-ago morning. Joseph had built it as a frame for the tomb in which his body would rest when his life was over. Seen in the faint light of first dawn, the garden was like a return to Eden.

Joseph had wealth and influence. He was a member of the Sanhedrin, the august Jewish assembly that legislated for the chosen people. He may also have been a personal friend of Pontius Pilate, because St. Matthew tells us he "went boldly to the Procurator and asked for the body of Jesus."

Normally the body of Our Lord would have been buried in the unmarked grave of the two thieves, who had been crucified with Him. Joseph's intervention saved it from that fate. His respect for Christ had led him to offer his own tomb as a resting place for one he revered and loved.

The burial had to be swift. By the time the body had been taken down from the cross the sun was westering. At sundown all work must cease for the beginning of the holiest feast of the year. The body was tenderly washed while Joseph hurried to buy a linen sheet to wrap the body in and spices for its preservation. The head was bound up with a fine napkin.

Then, carrying their burden down the slope, the sorrowful group, of which Christ's mother was undoubtedly one, walked through the garden and entered the vestibule of the tomb. Standing there, too torn by grief for tears, they watched while two of their number lifted the linen-shrouded figure, pathetically small in death, and settled it gently on the shallow shelf in the darkness of the inside room. The lights in their hands trembled with their emotion.

Coming out of the tomb, several men of the party must have pushed the massive stone, along the groove in which it moved like a millstone, until the door was completely closed. Then, carrying their burden of grief, the party dispersed. The stillness of the grave remained.

It was not long that the garden kept its quiet. The high priest and Pharisees who were responsible for the death of Jesus had been as active as Joseph.

They had gone to Pilate and demanded that a guard be authorized to keep watch over the tomb. So carefully had their malice and envy sifted every saying of Jesus that they now remembered He had once said, "After three days I shall rise again." It would be easy, the High Priest maintained, for the disciples to steal the body away before the three days were up, and then pretend that Christ had risen as He promised. In this way, they would perpetuate the influence of the "impostor" who claimed to be God's Son.

Pilate, a little tired of the whole affair by now, it would appear, looked at the fanatic group with cold eyes. When he spoke it was in abrupt phrases: "You have a guard, go make it secure as ye know how." Surely, if they had accomplished their objective of getting Christ crucified against Pilate's attempts to save Him, the guarding of a tomb should be a simple matter.

So officials were sent with a file of Roman soldiers, tradition says. They shattered the peace of the little garden, and with their heavy sandals probably trod down the flowers there. We may be sure that they were careful enough to move the great stone from the door. Entering the vestibule, they made sure that the linen-shrouded body of Christ was on its narrow shelf.

After they had rolled the stone back into place, the appointed officials sealed it with the great seal of the Sanhedrin, and the soldiers were once more instructed to guard the doorway carefully. The officials departed, secure in their importance and the conviction that they had closed the last door on the fame and power of Jesus.

It would be interesting to have heard the conversation of the soldiers after the officials departed. The Roman soldiers in Palestine were a rough and motley crew, recruited from the scum of the empire. To their coarse minds it must have seemed a joke that they should be assigned to guard a man who had been crucified. The execution had been public; death had been certain.

Some of the men probably pointed out that it wasn't such bad duty at all. The great Sabbath had arrived with sunset. Everything a soldier wanted would be shut down until the feast was over. By rotating the men on duty they would have time to rest a little and put their gear in order for the next inspection.

Yet, being what they were, men of primitive mentality and emotion, there must have been other thoughts at the back of their minds. Fear of the dead, perhaps, in this lonely place. Or stories of this man's life which were common knowledge and even common gossip. People said He had cured the deaf and the blind; He had made the lame walk. It was even said that He had brought the dead back to life. There was that widow's son that lived in Naim. And His friend Lazarus. What if this Jesus were to come back to life?

But it could not be. They had, during their years of service, seen death in every form. They knew that dead men were dead men, and they stayed dead. To think otherwise was foolish. At least they could hope for leave and more exciting duty when this dreary task was over.

The monotonous hours passed. The great city behind its towered walls became like the tomb they guarded. The walls of the exalted temple on the mountain caught the morning light on its polished marble pillars and its pinnacles of gold.

The soldiers went off guard and on again. Small fires were lit to cook their food, and at night for warmth. They talked of their experiences in the field and far places, laughing, joking, and trying to impress each other. They were probably glad that this assignment would soon be over, and more firmly convinced than ever that dead men stayed dead.

It was in the dim light, just before dawn, that it happened. Drowsy with their long vigil, the soldiers huddled about the door of the tomb. Suddenly the earth shook. They cried to each other in alarm. A loud noise deafened them; it was not like a roll of thunder but something unique, a sound never heard before. It was the clash of the gates of death, for the first time opening outward by the power within them.

While they watched in terror, the huge stone at the entrance to the tomb was wrenched back by a great angel like a flash of lightning coming from heaven above. The stone toppled and fell on the grass. The angel seated himself on it in glittering state.

At the entrance of the tomb, in the brief moments before the light blinded them, the soldiers probably saw a flash brighter than a thousand suns. In its center was the glittering form of a man glowing like the fires of the rainbow. His face from which light rayed like lightning was of a terrible and exalted beauty not of this world.

Completely blinded and terrified the soldiers fell on the grass and hid their faces. When they could see again, they scrambled to their feet and ran in panic toward the gates of Jerusalem. From St. Matthew we learn that the frightened soldiers were bribed to say that while they slept the disciples of Christ had stolen His body.

Actually, we have no description of the resurrection. St. Matthew gives us the clues of the angel and his snow-white robes, the earthquake and the stone rolled back and torn from its moorings so that the angel was able to sit on it. As in the birth of Our Lord, the evangelists are reticent to describe mysteries at which they were not present. Their restraint is a further proof of their truth-telling, if further proof were necessary. Yet we need to picture the resurrection if we are to make our hearts realize the power and glory of the risen Jesus.

He did not come forth from the tomb like a tremendous jinni of Oriental fairy tales. He arose as a man in a body fit to do the work of the glorified; impassible, rayed with light. In that moment of triumph for Him, and us as His adopted sons, His godhead flashed forth, and it was by His own power that He emerged glorious and immortal.

The angel remained as nunciate and messenger in the dramatic events that were to follow the resurrection. Something of his brightness was apparently veiled in order that He might not frighten those who were already coming out of Jerusalem in the dim morning light.

Who were the first to hear the news?

St. John says, "a group of women." St. Luke refers to them as "Mary Magdalene, Joanna and Mary the mother of James." St. Matthew puts the name of "Salome," instead of "Joanna," and St. Matthew says it was "Mary Magdalene and the other Mary."

The gospels were written not as scientific documents but as simple stories, recast from the accounts of those who were nearest to the events and still living when the gospels began to circulate. It is not astonishing that there should be minor discrepancies in these accounts, such as seeming confusion of names and numbers in this moment of unbearable excitement.

Three of the evangelists include the name of Mary Magdalene, and St. John further reports a beautiful incident about her which establishes her as the first person to behold the Lord in His risen body, though we must not rule out a prior appearance to His own, tenderly loved Mother.

It seems likely indeed that such a visit did take place, because of the love this Mother and her Son had for each other. Perhaps the evangelists did not record it because it was too intimate and sacred an occasion to be set down in the formal record that enshrined the story of the fulfillment of the prophecies of the Old Testament and the emergence of the Kingdom of God, not as it was thought to be by those who conceived of it as power and glory, but as Christ conceived it "in spirit and in truth." Neither are the private details of Our Lord's birth given by the evangelists. The reticence of the sacred writers about details of the actual resurrection is another instance of their respect for intimate and mysterious things.

If we imagine Mary praying on that morning of the resurrection, her Son was present to her heart in the same way that God was, since He is God. She who called herself "the slave of God" could accept the will of God with dignity and fortitude worthy of her high station. Her sorrow that He must suffer would be the sorrow in any mother's heart that one beautiful and innocent and helpless should be given over to the frightening cruelty of men.

Now all that was over. In Christ's glorified body His Mother could see the splendor of what it meant to do the will of His Father. His beauty, so torn and ravaged a few days ago, was reborn in a dazzling fashion that could no longer know death or sorrow.

So they would meet in joy and gladness, their embrace serene in its holiness and wordless understanding, like the joy of the mystics in union with God. Mary Magdalene might agonize at the foot of the cross and on the morning of the resurrection, but no word is said of Christ's Mother on both occasions because of her holiness, her position, and the respect accorded her by the evangelists. The record of the other actors in the sacred drama of Easter is marked with less altitude, as we can see in pursuing our story.

It is sufficient for the moment that we take the facts as St. Mark reports them to us in the Easter gospel we have heard so many times.

As St. Mark pictures it, we see Mary Magdalene, Mary the mother of James, and Salome, walking out of the city toward the sepulcher. It is clear that these loving women have worried all through the Passover about the hurried burial of Jesus. In their eyes it was not becoming to His eminence and dignity. With this thought in mind, they probably used all their ready money to buy precious spices and perfumes for a more decent anointing of One they loved and could never forget.

The dawn was beginning to show, a faint bar of gold on the horizon. Then, as they walked up the hill, one of the women asked an important question, "Who will roll away the stone from the entrance of the tomb?"

They hadn't thought of that important necessity in the haste of their concern.

When the three women arrived at the entrance, they were overjoyed to see that someone had already rolled back the stone, which had fallen on the grass. They entered the vestibule of the tomb and saw the angel sitting there, and they were terrified.

The angel told them not to be afraid. "Ye seek Jesus of Nazareth, who was crucified. He is risen, He is not here." The angel then bade them look into the tomb and see for themselves that it was empty, and then commanded them to tell the disciples and, most important of all, Peter, that Christ would see them in Galilee, as He had promised them.

After leaving the tomb, St. Mark says, they were seized "with trembling and amazement. And they told naught to any man, for they were afraid."

At this point St. Mark's narrative is broken. The events following the resurrection are telescoped in a hurried fashion greatly at variance with Mark's usual graphic style and method.

According to tradition, St. Mark was St. Peter's closest co-worker. In writing his gospel St. Mark used material from St. Peter's instructions to Roman converts. This gives rise to an interesting speculation. Could it be possible that St. Peter himself corrected and added the final section of Mark's gospel as a sort of brief summary of Christ's appearances to the disciples after the resurrection, concluding with the ascension of Our Lord? This would help to explain the telescoping of events. It would also explain the enigmatic statement in the telescoped section that Our Lord "first appeared to Mary Magdalene, out of whom He had cast seven devils," and would bring this statement into some sort of logical relationship with the complete story of Mary Magdalene told by St. John and the earlier story in Mark of her journey to the tomb with the other women.

One of two things is possible: either Mary Magdalene didn't enter the tomb with the other two women, or if she did one glance was sufficient to show her that the body was gone. There was one thing to do and Mary did it. She ran to tell Peter and John the alarming story.

The further story of Mary Magdalene, as St. John tells it, is informed with high drama. The other women at the tomb are not even mentioned by name. Mary Magdalene, because of her importance, is given the entire spotlight.

"Now on the first day of the week Mary Magdalene cometh early, while it is yet dark, unto the tomb; and she seeth the stone taken away from the tomb. She runneth therefore and cometh to Simon Peter and to the other disciple, whom Jesus loved, and saith to them, 'They have taken away the Lord out of the tomb, and we know not where they have laid Him.'

"Peter therefore went out, and the other disciple, and they went toward the tomb. And both ran together: and the other disciple outran Peter and came first to the tomb: and stooping down to look in, he seeth the linen cloths lying there, yet he went not in. Simon Peter therefore cometh also, following him, and went into the tomb; and he beholdeth the linen cloths lying there, while the napkin which had been upon His head was not lying with the linen cloths, but was rolled up apart in a place by itself. Then therefore the other disciple, who had come first to the tomb, also went in: and he saw and believed: for as yet they knew not the Scripture, that He must rise again from the dead. The disciples therefore went away again to their home.

"But Mary stood at the tomb without, weeping. Whilst therefore she was weeping, she stooped down and looked into the tomb, and she beholdeth two angels in white, sitting one at the head, and the other at the feet, where the body of Jesus had lain. And they say to her, 'Woman, why weepest thou?'

"She saith to them, 'Because they have taken away my Lord, and I know not where they have laid Him.'

"When she had said this, she turned around, and beholdeth Jesus standing, and she knew not that it was Jesus. Jesus saith to her, 'Woman, why weepest thou? Whom seekest thou?'

"She, thinking Him to be the gardener, saith to Him, 'Sir, if thou hast carried Him away, tell me where thou hast laid Him, and I will remove Him.'

"Jesus saith to her, 'Mary!'

"She turned and saith to Him in Hebrew, 'Rabboni!'—that is to say, 'Master!'

"Jesus saith to her, 'Hold Me not; for I have not yet ascended to the Father. But go to My brethren, and say to them, I ascend to My Father and your Father, to My God and your God.' "

"Mary Magdalene cometh announcing to the disciples that she hath seen the Lord, and that He said these things to her." JOHN XX, 1-18.

St. John's narrative, quoted above, helps to clear up some of the time relationships between this episode and the Easter story as related by St. Mark. Mary Magdalene did go to the tomb with the other two women. Seeing that it was empty, Mary ran from the tomb to find St. Peter and St.

John, the beloved disciple. Her words to the apostles were a cry filled with grief. "They have taken our Lord out of the tomb, and we know not where they have laid Him."

The "*we* know not" presumes the presence of the other women who were with her. It also presumes that Mary did not hear the angel's words, "He is risen, He is not here," or if she heard them she was too excited to understand them. In her anguish at seeing the winding-sheet and the napkin there, but not the body of her Lord, she could only think of finding Him again, as soon as possible. This one idea dominated her completely, until her anguish was amazingly resolved.

Her words to Peter and John communicated her excitement to them, and the two apostles ran from the city toward the tomb. Peter and John started out together, but John being much younger ended by completely outdistancing Peter and arrived breathless in the little garden before the tomb. John was polite enough to wait for his companion, though he did peer into the tomb and see the grave-cloths lying there.

When Peter arrived John followed him inside. We may presume that they carefully examined the sheet and the napkin. There is no angel indicated and no message. Our Lord put His two favorite apostles to a sterner test than the women, and the apostles came through it with flying colors. Now they remembered that He said He would rise from the dead after three days. They believed it completely, with hearts and minds, and returned to Jerusalem, overwhelmed with joy, eager to bring the good tidings to all the disciples.

Mary was still obsessed with the idea of trying to find the body of Jesus. Probably she had reached the tomb after Peter and John had returned to Jerusalem. She stood outside the door bitterly weeping, until she got courage to look inside the tomb once more, hoping against hope to see again the body of her Lord.

This time she saw two angels, but obviously her eyes, blurred with tears, failed to recognize them for what they were. When the angels asked her why she was weeping, Mary told them it was because she couldn't find the body of Jesus.

Having stated her case she was too impatient to wait for their announcement. Turning from the door of the tomb she saw Our Lord. He, too, asked her why she was weeping. Mary, either because of her obsession or her tear-blinded eyes, failed to recognize Jesus. She thought He might be Joseph of

Arimathea's gardener, and she begged Him to tell her where he had put the sacred body, if he had carried it away elsewhere.

From the details given in all the appearances of Our Lord after His resurrection, it is clear that His glorified body differed considerably from His normal appearance before death. This difference may have contributed to the fact that Mary failed to recognize Him at once. However, we must remember that Mary was looking for a *dead body*, not a living Saviour. Blind as she was from weeping, it would be difficult for her to see clearly all those loved things about Him which were so dear to her.

In any event, Our Lord brought the Magdalene out of her sorrow by the use of one word, "Mary," probably said with just the affectionate tone He had always used in pronouncing her name.

In a flash Mary comprehended the full meaning of the mystery—He was living, not dead. Uttering a great cry "Master," in which so much more of love is implied, Mary fell on her knees. Knowing her as we do, we may be sure that she was beside herself with joy; so much so, that Our Lord asked her to restrain it.

All that passed between Mary and Jesus is not found in the gospels. He must have enlightened her, consoled her, and given her the important task of telling the glad news to the disciples.

So far, on that first Easter morning, the facts of the resurrection had been revealed to several women. Mary Magdalene had actually seen the Master, probably because Jesus pitied her great sorrow and confusion of heart, that sprang from her intense love of Him.

It is easy to imagine that, aside from Peter and John, who believed at once the moment they saw the grave-clothes, many of the disciples of Our Lord and perhaps some apostles too were not much impressed with all this woman-talk. The case of Thomas offers good proof of this.

"The evening therefore of that same day, the first of the week, the doors of the place where the disciples were gathered being closed for fear of the Jews, Jesus came and stood in their midst, and saith to them, 'Peace be to you!'

"And when He had said this, He showed them His hands and His side. The disciples therefore rejoiced upon seeing the Lord. Jesus therefore said to them again, 'Peace be to you. As the Father hath sent Me, I also send you.'

"And when He had said this, He breathed upon them and saith to

them, 'Receive ye the Holy Ghost: whose sins ye shall forgive, they are forgiven them: whose sins ye shall retain, they are retained.'

"But Thomas, one of the Twelve, called the Twin, was not with them
when Jesus came. The other disciples therefore said to him, 'We have seen
the Lord.'

"But he said to them, 'Unless I see in His hands the print of the nails,
and put my finger into the place of the nails, and put my hand into His side,
I will not believe.'

"And after eight days, His disciples were again within, and Thomas with
them. Jesus cometh, the doors being closed, and stood in their midst, and
said, 'Peace be to you.'

"Then he saith to Thomas, 'Reach hither thy finger, and see My hands,
and reach hither thy hand and put it into My side; and be not unbelieving,
but believing.'

"Thomas answered and said to Him, 'My Lord and my God!'

"Jesus saith to him, 'Because thou hast seen Me, thou hast believed;
blessed are they that have not seen and have believed.' " JOHN XX, 19-29.

The disciples were probably afraid that the Sanhedrin were going to per-
secute them as they had persecuted Christ. As they waited in fear and confusion, with the doors of their assembly place bolted against the authorities, they
suddenly saw Jesus standing in their midst.

He greeted them with the salutation of peace as if to quiet all their fears
and the discussions about the morning's revelations. Then He held out His
pierced hands to them and pointed to the wound in His side in order that
they might know he was Christ crucified. We may be certain that there was
great rejoicing.

When silence had fallen in the amazed and admiring throng, Our Lord,
once more wished them peace of heart and gave them their commission to
convert the whole world. Then breathing upon them He invoked the Holy
Spirit and gave them power over sinners, "whose sins ye shall forgive they
are forgiven them: whose sins ye shall retain they are retained."

At this point St. John inserts the story of the doubting Thomas as an example of the type of hard-headed men Our Lord had to convince that He
was risen. The story is also a warning to us not to follow the example of
Thomas.

The final episodes which round out the story of God's first Sunday give us clues regarding the state of mind of many of the disciples. St. Luke places the first event sometime in the afternoon.

"And behold, that very day, two of them were on their way to a village named Emmaus, a hundred and sixty furlongs distant from Jerusalem, and were talking one with another over all these events. And it came to pass that whilst they were talking and discussing, Jesus himself drew nigh and went along with them; but their eyes were held that they should not recognize Him. He said unto them, 'What words are these that ye exchange one with another as ye walk along?'

"And they stood still, with gloomy looks; and one of them, named Cleophas, answered and said unto Him, 'Thou alone sojournest in Jerusalem and knowest not the things that have happened therein in these days?'

"And He said to them, 'What things?'

"They said to Him, 'Concerning Jesus of Nazareth, Who was a prophet, mighty in work and word before God and all the people; and our high priests and rulers delivered Him up to be condemned to death and crucified Him. Ourselves were hoping that it was He who should redeem Israel. Yea, and besides all this it is now the third day since these things befell; and moreover certain women of ours have amazed us, who went at dawn to the tomb, and found not His body, but came saying that they had even seen a vision of angels, who say that He is alive. So some of our company went off to the tomb, and they found that it was even as the women had said, but Him they saw not.'

"But He said unto them, 'O senseless men, and slow of heart to believe in all that the prophets have spoken! Ought not the Christ to have suffered these things, and thus enter into His glory?'

"And beginning from Moses and all the prophets He expounded for them in all the scriptures the things about Himself.

"And they drew nigh to the village whither they were going, and Himself made as though he would go further; and they pressed Him, saying, 'Stay with us, for evening approacheth and already the day declineth.'

"So He went to stay with them. And it came to pass when He reclined at table with them, that He took the bread and blessed and brake and handed it to them. And their eyes were opened, and they recognized Him; and He vanished from them. And they said one to another, 'Was not our heart burning within us whilst He spoke to us on the way, whilst He laid open to us the scriptures?'" LUKE XXIV, 13-32.

In other words, the risen Lord came on two of the seventy-two disciples walking toward Emmaus, a village probably six or seven miles from Jerusalem. One of the disciples was named Cleophas. The other is not identified.

They were discussing the crucifixion and all the talk of women that Christ had risen. Apparently from their gloomy looks they were discouraged and unbelieving. Why should Christ reveal His resurrection to a few women and not show Himself to the apostles or disciples? In the Hebrew world, where men are everything, the whole affair seemed suspect.

Christ joined Cleophas and his companion but they failed to recognize Him, either because of some divine intervention or that strange change in His glorified body.

Our Lord let them reveal the confused and unbelieving state of their minds before turning on them with the rebuke, "O senseless men, and slow of heart to believe in all the prophets have spoken."

He followed the stern rebuke with a picture taken from Moses and the prophets which completely described the Messias as one who would appear, teach, be put to death and rise again, as Christ did. In doing so, Our Lord shattered the false hope of Cleophas and his companion that Christ was to be a powerful ruler, and that His kingdom was to be like worldly kingdoms. The disciples hadn't believed the holy women because they hadn't searched the scriptures, either thoroughly or correctly.

Such was the power of Our Lord's explanation that the hearts of the two disciples burned with fervor. They wanted to hear more; they could listen forever to this stranger.

So, as evening was coming on, they asked Him to dine with them, obviously hoping to hear more. Once seated at the table the stranger broke bread before them with the particular blessing Jesus had always used. Suddenly they knew. Their eyes were opened. It was Jesus Who was their companion, it was He who had instructed them and now sat in their midst, with His pierced hands breaking the bread!

They had been running away from Jerusalem, but now, after the Lord "vanished," they rushed back to the Holy City to tell the apostles and disciples, gathered in the upper room, very likely, "in fear of the Jews," a scene St. John has already described for us.

It is particularly important for us to recall St. Luke's description of the episode, because the story as he presents it with meticulous realism is the climax to a day of wonder and importance.

"And that very hour they arose and returned to Jerusalem, where they found the eleven gathered together and those that were with them, saying, 'The Lord is risen indeed and hath appeared to Simon.'

"And themselves recounted what had befallen on their journey, and how they had recognized Him at the breaking of the bread.

"Now whilst they were speaking these things, Himself stood in their midst and saith to them, 'Peace be to you!'

"But they were terrified and stricken with fear, and thought that they beheld a spirit. And He said to them, 'Why are ye troubled, and wherefore do doubts arise in your heart? See My hands and My feet, that it is My very self. Feel Me and see, for a spirit hath not flesh and bones, as ye see Me to have.'

"And saying this, He showed them His hands and His feet. But as they still disbelieved for very joy and marvelled, He said to them, 'Have you aught here to eat?'

"They handed Him part of a broiled fish; and He took and ate before them.

"And He said unto them, 'These are My words which I spoke unto you whilst I was yet with you, even that all the things that are written in the Law of Moses and the prophets and the psalms concerning Me must be fulfilled.'

"Then He opened their mind, that they might understand the scriptures. And He said to them, 'Thus it is written: that the Christ should suffer, and should rise from the dead on the third day, and that in His name should be preached repentance unto forgiveness of sins unto all the nations, beginning from Jerusalem. Yourselves are witnesses of these things. And behold, I send forth upon you the promise of My Father. But do ye bide in the city, until ye be clothed with power from on high.' " LUKE XXIV, 33-49.

Thus Cleophas and his companion told their story to the apostles and disciples, and Jesus appeared and drove home to the apostles and disciples the truths He had been explaining to Cleophas and his friend in Emmaus.

Before doing so, He calmed their fears. He also proved to them that He was still the same person He was before He was crucified by showing them the five wounds and asking them to feel for themselves His body of flesh and bones.

Seeing that they were still overcome with joy and amazement, Our Lord ate, conferred on them the grace of understanding, and bade them search the Scriptures where they would find it written, "That the Christ should suffer, and should rise from the dead on the third day, and that in His name should be preached repentance unto forgiveness of sins unto all the nations."

Our risen Lord's final command was that they were to remain in Jerusalem until the coming of the Holy Ghost.

Such is the story of the resurrection as we find it in the New Testament —a story of joy such as the world had never known until Christ rose triumphantly from the dead. With the dawning of this day there stretched out for man the vistas of a new spiritual Eden, and the possibility of radiant immortality.

Christ rose from the dead, His body glorified. In His resurrection is the promise of ours. We too, at the end of time, in Him and with Him, will assume glorified flesh in the resurrection of our bodies as Christ promises. "O grave where is thy victory? O death where is thy sting?" St. Paul cries out.

The first fulfillment of that promise is found in Our Lady. Through the paths of lightways her Son came one morning, took her by the hand and raised her to heaven, glorious and immortal. "She in us and we in her are beating Godward," as the poet Francis Thompson has said.

Looking at that first Easter in the gospels, we discover many deep things we can learn to use in deepening ourselves.

Love finds Christ in the shortest time and by the shortest way. The women who came to pour out their anointing perfumes on the body of the Saviour were the first to hear the glad tidings.

Mary Magdalene, whose heart was anguished with sorrow, was the first to see Him in His glorified flesh. Much was forgiven her, and much was *given* her, because she had loved much.

Along with love, we learn the lesson of faith in Christ's promises. Peter and John came to the tomb after talking to Mary Magdalene. They found the door of the tomb open; they saw and examined the shroud of Our Lord and the napkin that bound up His head. They recalled His promise that He would rise from the dead. Small though the evidence was, their hearts were flooded with belief.

How unlike the holy women, how unlike Peter and John, were many of the disciples: the two on the way to Emmaus, the doubting Thomas and all those in our own time, ourselves perhaps, who reason away Our Lord's miracles and that greatest miracle of them all—the resurrection. Love and faith—the paths to God most obvious!

There is also the command for all of us, both the strong and the weak. *Search the scriptures!* Read them often; meditate upon them. See that they are like illuminated manuscripts shouting the beauty of God, telling us the glorious things of the Old Testament that His life in the New Testament reveals in its radiant fullness: the shadow and the substance of God made man.

O Holy Mother, teach us to search the Scriptures even as you did, bringing out of them the poetry and praise of God. Teach us your faith in God's power. Teach us your love that saw in His resurrection the glory that came to you and will come to all of us in the resurrection of the body. Help us to look forward to that glorious day through all the shadows of time, now and at the hour of our death.

THE SECOND
GLORIOUS MYSTERY

The Ascension

"To them also He showed Himself alive after His passion by many proofs, during forty days appearing to them and speaking of the kingdom of God. And while at table with them He charged them not to depart from Jerusalem, but to await the promise of the Father, 'whereof ye have heard from Me; for John baptized with water, but ye shall be baptized with the Holy Spirit not many days hence.'

"They therefore that were assembled asked Him, saying, 'Lord, wilt Thou at this time restore the kingdom to Israel?'

"He said to them: 'It is not for you to know times or seasons which the Father hath appointed by His own authority; but ye shall receive power from the coming of the Holy Spirit upon you, and ye shall be My witnesses in Jerusalem, and in all Judaea and Samaria, and unto the end of the earth.'

"And when He had said these things, He was lifted up before their eyes, and a cloud received Him out of their sight. And while they were gazing at the heaven as He went, behold, two men stood by them in white garments, who said: 'Men of Galilee, why stand ye looking into heaven? This Jesus, Who hath been taken up from you into heaven, will come after the same manner wherein ye have beheld Him going into heaven.'

"Then they returned unto Jerusalem from Mount Olivet, as it is called, which is near Jerusalem, a sabbath journey away." Acts I, 3-12.

The passion, death and resurrection of Our Lord were over, with their high drama, piercing sorrow, and exalted joy. Yet for forty days Christ lived on earth in His risen body. Day after day the disciples saw Him in all the

postures of their life together. The most skeptical among them, the most re-
luctant to believe, were forced to admit to themselves that it was the same Lord
and Master as of old, but different in that His beauty now shone forth like a
star, His gravity was now informed with majestic command.

Formerly, in their years together, walking the dusty roads, sleeping under
the stars, straining at the nets, He had said things to them that sounded like
high doctrine, but the occasions on which He spoke wore the masks of
enigma. They were thinking of one thing, while He was talking of another.

They were all convinced He was a born leader, a king fit to unite their
people and bring back again the golden age of Solomon. It had seemed of
some moment to discover who would sit on His right and left hand, sharing
the rule of the kingdom; it had seemed of some moment to angle for honors,
as some of the apostles did. The multiplication of loaves in the desert and
the raising of Lazarus had been ultimate signs of His power to achieve the
impossible. They seemed to presage a rule more powerful and more universal
than men had ever dreamed.

This dream had been rudely shattered that fateful night in the olive garden. Confronted there, in the torchlight, He had held out His hands instead
of striking down those evil men who had come to kill Him. Watching the
ignominy of the cross the following day they had again waited a shattering
sign. It had not been given.

They could see now, in the light of His resurrection, how wrong they
had been in their understanding of His kingdom. It was an interior kingdom:
in the world but *not* of it. There came back to them the echoes of doctrines
He had taught: of meekness, of purity and of peace. In the radiance of His
risen countenance the dark places in their minds were beginning to open up
to light.

It is in trying to read the minds of the disciples of Our Lord after the
resurrection that we come to a more complete understanding of the gospels
which bring the story to us.

Before the resurrection Jesus spoke to the disciples as teacher and leader,
but He spoke as the first among them—one of themselves. His teaching
seemed mysterious to them, full of riddles. What He said fell on ears only a
little less deaf than those of Judas.

After the resurrection they could detect in every movement of His body,
in every flash of His eyes, that He was what He was. On the very day of His

resurrection, while they were still partly bewildered and unbelieving, He had given them authority over forgiveness. "Whose sins you shall forgive they are forgiven them; whose sins you shall retain they are retained."

Their enormous respect for what was so obvious in His appearance had made them diffident. The old intimate approach to Jesus seemed presumptuous; reverence, tinged with fear, had taken its place. And it was in this state of mind, after His astonishing appearances to them in Jerusalem, that the eleven disciples went into Galilee to the mountain rendezvous Jesus had appointed.

Was it the hill where He had once taught the people the way to life, while the blue waters behind them mirrored the sky? We do not know, since the gospels do not give us the precise information.

St. Matthew presents us with one episode of the complete story.

After the apostles had reached the appointed place, Christ appeared to them. "They worshipped Him," Matthew says, "but some still remained in doubt of what He was and what their part in the kingdom was to be."

Jesus went directly to their difficulties with a command that largely removed their doubts and perplexities: "All power in heaven and on earth hath been given Me. Go ye, therefore, make disciples of all the nations, baptizing them in the name of the Father and of the Son and of the Holy Spirit: teaching them to observe all that I have commanded you: and behold, I am with you all days, unto the consummation of the world." MATTHEW XXVIII, 18-20.

The declaration of His godhead was precise in the opening phrases. Equally astounding was what followed it. They had all thought the coming kingdom had been restricted to the Jews alone. Now it was clear that it would embrace all nations and all peoples. And discipleship was to be signalized by a baptism, such as John preached, but it was to be under the triple names of the Son Who stood before them, the Father Who sent Him, and the Holy Spirit Who was yet to come, as Jesus had told them in His last solemn charge at their supper the night before His death.

The commands He had given them in the three years of His teaching were to be the rules of a new life for all. This they could now see in the light of the new conception and meaning of the kingdom. How He should be with them all days until the consummation of the world was more mysterious; but since He had fulfilled all that He had promised them, how could they doubt it?

To these amazing instructions about the kingdom found in St. Matthew, St. Mark has something to add, a clear-cut pronouncement, as terrifying as it is clear.

"And He said to them, 'Go ye into all the world and preach the gospel to the whole creation. He that believeth and is baptized shall be saved: he that believeth not shall be condemned. And these signs shall follow them that believe: in My name they shall cast out devils, they shall speak with new tongues, and they shall take up serpents in their hands, and if they drink any deadly thing it shall not harm them: they shall lay hands upon the sick and they shall recover.'" MARK XVI, 15-18.

Those who will not believe are rejected. Those who believe and are baptized shall be saved. And God will work wonders through His disciples, that men may have positive signs that their work is from God.

Matthew and Mark give us the first news of the world-wide kingdom imparted to the Apostles, with absolute authority, somewhere in the forty days Jesus remained on earth after His resurrection.

St. John records one more incident to round out the picture. Pictorially, it is one of the most thrilling events to be found in the gospels. It is something far more than that, however. It is meant to be the crown and completion of the instructions Jesus had already given the disciples in Matthew and Mark, and it is presented with intimacy and loving-kindness, which set it apart as symbolic of the love of Jesus for His Apostles, and for all men who love Him.

"After these things, Jesus manifested Himself again to the disciples by the Sea of Tiberias; and He manifested Himself in this way. There were together Simon Peter, and Thomas, called the Twin, and Nathanael from Cana in Galilee, and the sons of Zebedee, and two other of His disciples. Simon Peter saith to them, 'I go a-fishing.'

"They say to him, 'We also are coming with thee.'

"They went forth and entered into the ship; and that night they took nothing. But at break of day Jesus stood on the shore; yet the disciples knew not that it was Jesus. Jesus therefore saith to them, 'Children, have ye any fish?'

"They answered Him, 'No.'

"And He said to them, 'Cast the net to the right side of the ship, and ye shall find.'

"They cast therefore, and now they were not able to haul it in for the multitude of the fish. That disciple therefore whom Jesus loved saith to Peter, 'It is the Lord.'

"When Simon Peter therefore heard that it was the Lord, he girt his tunic about him (for he was naked), and cast himself into the sea. But the other disciples came with the boat, dragging the net full of fish; for they were not far from land, but about a hundred yards off. When therefore they had landed, they see a fire there, and a fish laid thereon, and bread. Jesus saith to them, 'Bring some of the fish which ye have now taken.'

"Simon Peter therefore went aboard and drew the net to land, full of great fish, one hundred and fifty-three in number; and although there were so many, the net was not rent.

"Jesus saith to them, 'Come and breakfast.'

"None of the disciples durst ask Him, 'Who art thou?', knowing that it was the Lord. Jesus cometh and taketh the bread and giveth to them, and the fish in like manner.

"Thus was Jesus manifested now a third time to the disciples, after He had risen from the dead.

"When therefore they had breakfasted, Jesus saith to Simon Peter, 'Simon, son of John, lovest thou Me more than do these?'

"He saith to Him, 'Yea, Lord, Thou knowest that I love Thee.'

"He saith to him, 'Feed My lambs.'

"He saith to him again a second time, 'Simon, son of John, lovest thou Me?'

"He saith to Him, 'Yea, Lord, Thou knowest that I love Thee.'

"He saith to him, 'Shepherd My sheep.'

"He saith to him a third time, 'Simon, son of John, lovest thou Me?'

"Peter was grieved because He said to him the third time, 'Lovest thou Me?' And he said to Him, 'Lord, Thou knowest all things; Thou knowest that I love Thee.'

"Jesus saith to him, 'Feed My sheep. Amen, amen, I say to thee, when thou wast young, thou didst gird thyself, and didst walk whither thou wouldst; but when thou shalt be old, thou shalt stretch forth thy hands, and another shall gird thee and lead thee whither thou wouldst not.'

"Now this He said signifying by what manner of death he should glorify God." JOHN XXI, 1-19.

The scene described above is a beautiful one—a blue morning on the Sea of Tiberias. This select group of disciples had found it necessary to pursue their trade during the time they were seeing Christ and were being instructed by Him. After fishing all night, they must have been discouraged, for they had not caught a single fish.

Suddenly they beheld a strange figure standing on the shore, a hundred yards away. He asked them if they had any fish and they shouted back, "No." He told them to drop their net to the right of the ship. They started hauling it in and found it simply bursting with fish.

This miraculous catch of fish at once reminded St. John of that other morning long ago when Jesus had worked the same wonder for them. This stranger on the shore—it must be Jesus.

John immediately told Peter, "It's the Lord." Without waiting a moment, the impetuous Peter, who had been fishing clad only in a loin cloth, girded his tunic about him and, half-wading, half-swimming, hurried toward the shore. The others followed him as fast as they could in the boat, dragging the bulging net behind them.

They must have been delighted to discover that Jesus had already kindled a fire. The smell of the toasting bread and broiling fish was welcome to their nostrils, but thrice welcome that it revealed His love and thought for them. Except for the majestic appearance of the Lord, it was quite like the old days. Jesus greeted them casually and commanded them to bring some of the fish they had caught.

Peter, as the master of the boat, superintended the drawing of the net and the counting of the fish. They exclaimed over the catch. Then Jesus broke in on their preoccupation with the command, "Come and breakfast."

At this point in the narration St. John has a comment that ties in with what the other evangelists had said of the changed appearance of Jesus after His resurrection. St. John says, "None of the disciples durst ask Him, 'Who art Thou?', knowing that it was the Lord."

This clue is a further expression of the new majesty and authority clothing Our Lord. They could see it was Jesus from the pierced hands and feet, but there was something awesome in that beloved face and the kingly way in which He held himself. Very likely they ate their food in silence; watching the play of light on the water and on the memorable face of Jesus.

They felt sure He had come to them for some precise purpose. Their surmise was correct, for the moment breakfast was over Jesus questioned Peter's great love for Him three times. Twice Peter answered with a strong affirmation, and twice he was commanded to feed and shepherd the flock of Christ.

When Jesus asked Peter the same question the third time, "Lovest thou Me?", Peter was sorrowful, remembering the night in which he had thrice denied his Master. He answered with an oblique tribute to the divinity of Christ. "Lord, Thou knowest all things; Thou knowest that I love Thee."

Our Lord the third time commanded the great apostle to feed His sheep, and then foretold the death of Peter with perhaps a small ironic comment on St. Peter's stubbornness.

The entire episode is beautifully human, wonderfully prophetic. It is the capstone to the other commands Jesus had already given them in His prior appearances. On the previous occasions He had told them the universal nature of His kingdom, the baptismal rite necessary for entrance into its fellowship, and the rite for the forgiveness of sins. In this appearance Christ imposed order in His kingdom by confirming Peter as the chief shepherd of the flock, and he drove His command home to the apostles by solemnity and reiteration.

In this fashion we can see that Christ's risen life on earth was a necessary prelude to the ascension.

For that scene, described at the beginning of this chapter, we may return to the Acts of the Apostles and the careful narration of St. Luke quoted earlier.

The last day of Christ's time on earth in His risen majesty had finally arrived. The apostles were all back in Jerusalem, sitting at the table with Jesus. We may well believe that the Mother of Our Lord was in the room with them. It is also probable that the meal was in the upper room, sacred to all of them since the night of the great Supper.

In the short hours remaining, before He must return to His Father, they were all looking at Him, trying to remember that face forever: as it was in the intimate three years of their training, before majesty clothed it with new meaning. They must have asked Jesus many questions, because they were still fearful about many things, still confused about the exact and entire meaning of the kingdom, as we shall see.

Finally Jesus, knowing the enlightenment they desired, and their stubborn preconceptions, solemnly charged them not to depart from Jerusalem, but to await the promise He had made them at the last supper, that they were all to be baptized soon in the Holy Spirit.

It must have been exasperating at this point, after all the explanations, the commands and instructions, that some of them asked the same foolish question, "Lord, wilt Thou at this time restore the kingdom to Israel?"

There it was—they still wanted their physical kingdom; they were still thinking of *Jewish good,* instead of the *universal good.*

There was a hint of rebuke in Our Lord's answer, "It is not for you to know the times or seasons which the Father hath appointed by His own authority." The rebuke was softened with the promise that if it was power they wished they should soon receive it from the Holy Spirit. It was this power which would enable them to give witness to Him in Jerusalem and the farthest corners of the earth. They were still worldly men, and the coming of the Holy Spirit would not only enlighten their minds to see exactly what the kingdom meant, but would spiritualize them and make them like lions in its pursuit.

Leaving the room at last, we may picture them as they walked out of the city toward Mount Olivet. Summer was all about them, rich with the promise of fulfillment in tree and shrub and flower. Along the way they exchanged confidences, the memorable three walking together, Jesus and His Mother and John, with Peter and the others following solemnly, talking in hushed voices.

Then, on the radiant mountain top, Jesus said His last farewells, joyous this time, but no less poignant in that they would see Him no more until they saw Him in the kingdom of His Father.

They watched Him, hands outstretched in benediction, being lifted into the luminous summer air—fading away before them.

Did His face shine like the sun? Were His garments whiter than snow, as on that day of Transfiguration, when He talked with Moses and Elias? St. Luke does not tell us—only that a cloud finally veiled the glorious presence.

But, though He was gone from their eyes, they still stared as if entranced into the sun-shot spaces of the sky. They were recalled to where they were by the sudden appearance of two angels clothed in white and wearing the form of men. There was reproach against idleness and sorrow in the angels' greeting: Christ who had left them in glory would return in clouds of glory to judge the world.

The risen Christ in His glorified humanity sat at the right hand of His Father. And the entire host of heaven welcomed Him in a paean of joy and light.

As summer is a time of nature's triumph, of harvest and fulfillment, the mood of the year is admirably suited to the feast of the Ascension. Now the Scriptures were fulfilled. Man is redeemed from original sin. Tragedy and sorrow have been turned into glory.

Christ, the architect of the new Eden, labored for forty days of dazzling majesty, telling His disciples what the kingdom was to be, and what were the rules for entrance into its holy order. The glory of those dazzling visions of the forty days deepened with His ascension, as He returned to the rule of the universe at the right hand of His Father. He had worn the mask of His humanity, with all that is implied of weariness, pain and sorrow, in doing the will of His Father in redeeming us. All these had now been wiped out in the glory of heaven, and the brooding of the Holy Spirit over the world.

O Holy Mother, teach us to look up to heaven where your Son reigns in glory. Teach us to see His kingdom of truth and holiness as He wished us to see it, with all its glorious implications for the world until its consummation. Keep us from being narrow: make us understand that His rule is for all, His sacraments the steps through time to our own glory. Help us to see that even as He ascended in power, He will come one day in power and majesty to judge the world. Help us to see through fear of judgment to our glory with Him. Now and at the hour of our death.

THE THIRD

GLORIOUS MYSTERY

The Descent of the Holy Ghost

"AND when the day of Pentecost was come, they were all gathered together in one place. And suddenly there came a noise from heaven, as of the rushing of a blast of wind, which filled the whole house where they were seated. And there appeared to them tongues, as though of fire, which parted and sat upon every one of them. And they were all filled with the Holy Spirit, and began to speak in foreign tongues, according as the Spirit gave them to utter.

"Now there were staying in Jerusalem devout Jews from every country under heaven; and when this sound befell, the multitude came together and was confounded, because each one heard them speaking his own language. And they were beside themselves with wonder, saying, 'Lo, are not all these who speak Galilaeans? How is it that we hear each our own language, wherein we were born? Parthians and Medes and Elamites, dwellers in Mesopotamia, Judaea and Cappadocia, in Pontus and Asia, in Phrygia and Pamphylia, in Egypt and the parts of Africa about Cyrene, and the visitors from Rome, yea, Jews and proselytes, Cretans and Arabians, we hear them speaking in our own tongues of the mighty works of God.'" ACTS OF THE APOSTLES, II, 1-11.

St. Luke wrote the Acts of the Apostles and dedicated it to Theophilus, the same patron to whom he had earlier dedicated his gospel. Little or nothing is known of him, but from the form of the address—"most excellent"—we may infer that he was an imperial Roman official. Politeness demanded the term "excellency," as it does today for high officials in government service.

The name Theophilus means "beloved of God." Because of this, some scriptural commentators have speculated that Theophilus symbolizes not a person, but all those beloved of God who have been received into the early Church, for the Acts, like St. Luke's gospel, seems to be directed toward the Gentile world from which the greatest number of converts was being made.

The Acts, sometimes called the "fifth gospel," is usually thought of as narrative history, and it tells us many of the things we know about the amazing growth of the Church in the first thirty years of her existence. In addition to this it brings us sharply-etched portraits of St. Peter, St. Paul and other important personages of apostolic times, along with the clash of their personalities and actions.

It would be a mistake, however, to presume that the Acts has little doctrinal content. The Christian faith, as one eminent commentator describes it, is "a piece of history, that of God's intervention in the affairs of mankind; and Acts is the only history we possess of the coming of the Holy Spirit, and His guidance of the Church during the first momentous thirty years."

Among the developing doctrines are the implicit and explicit teaching of the divinity of Christ and the clear emergence of the mystery of the Trinity, with its distinctions of three divine Persons and their specific actions on the world.

The Church is portrayed as an institution with an organized daily life, liturgy and sacraments. The primacy of St. Peter is also described in considerable detail in the Acts. We see all these things in action, as it were, but in such an unmistakable way that we are able to discern their entire meaning.

In the first chapter of the Acts, St. Luke gives us a summary of Our Lord's work among the Apostles during the forty days of His risen and glorified life on earth, climaxed with a poignant and dramatic account of the ascension of Our Lord into heaven. After that we observe the apostles, disciples and the holy women returning to the upper room of the Cenacle. The Blessed Virgin was with them and they "were persevering with one accord in prayer."

St. Peter then explained from the Scriptures that it was necessary to elect a new apostle to take the place of the renegade Judas who had hanged himself in despair. Two candidates were chosen from the seventy-two disciples, "Joseph called Barabbas," and Matthias. After a prayer, probably offered by St. Peter, lots were cast and Matthias became the twelfth apostle.

Having closed their ranks and prepared the way for the revelation of the Holy Spirit promised them by Christ at the last supper and in the forty days of His risen life on earth, we may well believe that they turned with still greater unity to prayer, in preparation for the coming event.

It happened on the feast of Pentecost, celebrated fifty days after the Passover. The feast had first been kept as a harvest festival in thanksgiving to God. Later it assumed a slightly different orientation as a yearly remembrance of the great gift of the law on Mount Sinai. It was a joyful feast: behind the bountiful harvests over the years was the harvest of the commandments that had made the Jewish people God's chosen ones. But Christ at the right hand of His Father had prepared a new gift and a new splendor that was to flow out like a mighty river touching all men and all races until the end of time. The reign of the Holy Spirit was about to begin.

The upper room on that Pentecost morning was wrapped in the silence of prayer. Seated there was the Mother of Jesus. The twelve were grouped about the room; each completely concentrated on God in his own individual fashion.

Suddenly a mighty wind shook the place. It was not like any wind they had ever heard before in their years of fishing and outdoor living. It seemed to be centered over the building in which they were praying. Its core was the upper room itself.

So unusual was the phenomenon that people in every section of Jerusalem, including men and women from all over the Roman world who had come up for the feast, started running through the crooked streets toward the building from which the roaring sound came.

The little group in the Cenacle were shaken out of themselves. Perhaps a wind of fear blew through their hearts, but even as it came, the upper reaches of the hall were lit with flame that separated into tongues of fire resting above the heads of Our Lady and the apostles, who had fallen on their knees in the presence of God, felt not only in the air above them, but poured like exotic wine through every bone and fiber of their being.

What it was like to experience this bath in God we do not know. Nor does St. Luke tell us what they felt in these flaming moments of Pentecost.

Great mystics like St. John of the Cross and Teresa of Avila have tried to describe experiences like this, but they do so in figures that mean different things to different people. For me the best expression of Pentecost and its inner meaning is to be found in a painting by El Greco. In it the Blessed Virgin, with hands folded in prayer, is seated in the center of the apostles and some of the holy women, who are gathered closely about her chair. In the foreground Peter and John are bent backward, half-unconscious with ecstasy. Tongues of flame float in the air above their heads, sent down from the Holy Spirit, at the top of the panel, in the form of a dove floating in a cloud of golden fire. The face of the Virgin is ecstatic, as if she, above all others, was at the very heart of the mystery, completely transfixed by heavenly love.

The whole feeling of this picture of Pentecost comes from a double movement. It is obvious that the primal motion downward emanates from the *lumen,* the insubstantial light that bathes them all in the radiance of things unseen. And the figures in the room respond with an upward movement of their bodies, carried out of themselves by the force pulling them heavenward.

St. Luke does not record how long the experience lasted, but its effects were immediate and astonishing. Transported out of themselves, the apostles and all those who had received the Holy Spirit began to chant the praises of God in many languages.

By this time a large crowd had gathered in the street court below. They were from all over the Roman empire, visitors, students and ordinary dwellers in Jerusalem. Yet, in spite of their different languages, each one of them heard one of the disciples speaking of God and His wonderful works in the language of his own country. Everyone in the crowd was astonished. Some asked each other what this miracle could possibly mean. Others scoffed at the wonder saying, "They are drunk with sweet wine."

While the hubbub was at its height, St. Peter, standing in their midst, began to speak to the multitude, probably in the common Greek they all understood because it was the international language of the period. What Peter said was important and astonishing. Even more miraculous was the change in him. Up to this point the gospels picture him as a rough-hewn, plain-speaking fisherman. He has had moments of inspiration, such as the day in which he was the first to hail Our Lord as "Christ the Son of the living

God." But under pressure he has appeared timid and uncertain, to the point of thrice denying Our Lord on the night Jesus was taken prisoner by the Sanhedrin. Now, after the descent of the Holy Spirit, Peter was a veritable lion. Now he spoke with decision and authority—in keeping with his position as chief of the apostles.

Without any rabbinic training whatever, he revealed under the direct inspiration of the Holy Ghost a masterly ability to interpret prophecy, clothed in subtle shades of thought and language. First he bluntly denied that they were drunk, as some had charged. His reasoning here had a touch of humor in it, in that he seemed to be asking his auditors "Who would be drunk on sweet wine at nine o'clock in the morning?"

Then he proceeded with his inspired sermon, explaining in the words of the prophet Joel that the last religious period had dawned, the period in which the Holy Spirit is poured out upon all men, leading them to prophecy and vision accompanied by extraordinary miracles and signs.

Peter next proceeded to prove from the psalms of David that the Lord meant by Joel is Jesus of Nazareth, Who rose from the dead and sits on the right hand of God in heaven as David had foretold. The prince of the apostles is emphatic that the crucified Jesus is both the Son of God and the promised Messias.

Peter's inspired sermon led his hearers to repentance for their guilt in being partially responsible for crucifying Christ. When they asked him for direction, Peter urged them to be baptized and wipe out their sins, and he promised them the gifts of the Holy Spirit such as they had seen exemplified that very morning in himself and the apostles. The offer of salvation is not only open to them who are listening but applies to the whole world "afar off," both Jew and Gentile.

St. Luke does not give the end of St. Peter's discourse, but he does tell us that with "many other words," he adjured and exhorted them saying, "Save yourselves from this perverse generation."

"They therefore that accepted what he said were baptized, and there were added that day about three thousand souls." It was certainly one of the most effective sermons in the whole history of preaching.

The marvelous descent of the Holy Spirit with all its extraordinary physical manifestations was over, but the quickening and strengthening effects remain, as St. Luke tells us: "And they persevered in the teaching of the apostles and the fellowship, the breaking of bread and the prayers. And fear fell upon every soul; and many wonders and signs were wrought through the apostles. And all they that had believed held all things in common together; and they used to sell their property and goods and distribute the price among all, according as anyone had need. Day by day they persevered with one accord in the temple, and breaking bread at home, they took food with joyful simplicity of heart, praising God and in favour with the whole people. And the Lord added to the company day by day those who were being saved." ACTS II, 42-47.

The mystery of Pentecost, like the birth and resurrection of Our Lord, is one of the most memorable of days in the history of the world. The entire Old Testament tells us about the work of the Father in creating the world and the stern molding of a people to His purposes. Rising above the turmoil and murk of those stark ancient days are the prophecies about the Redeemer and Sanctifier of man in an age of love to come. There they shine out above the darkness, like a garland of daystars telling the whole world that the darkness is almost past.

After Pentecost the days of promise were over. The heavens had opened with vivifying flame. The weak humanity of the apostles and disciples was exalted, illuminated and made strong for proclaiming the new age of love and the casting of the fiery gospel over the entire world.

The vigorous sermon of St. Peter is the Church in action: forever seeking, through sword and fire, persecution and death, the conquest of the world in the name of Jesus. It is not in activity alone, however, that perfection comes into being. At the core of souls and in the heart of the Church the Spirit broods in tranquility. In the sacraments and prayer the Christian community is drawn together in the bonds of love.

So prized was this unity in the days following Pentecost that some men of considerable wealth gave it all to the common treasury for works of charity. They never tired talking *of* Jesus, and talking *to* God in the holy places of the temple, and in the celebration of the Eucharist in their homes. They ate together and prayed together. So mild, tranquil and joyful were they that all Jerusalem commented on the fact, and began to inquire what it was that could inspire men with such unity and joy.

O Holy Mother, help us to love the Holy Spirit. Help us to cast His fire of love over the world. Keep our hearts tranquil and without sin that they may be fitting dwellings for the Spirit of God. Strengthen us to be eager in doing all we can to speed the kingdom on earth. Now and at the hour of our death.

THE FOURTH

GLORIOUS MYSTERY

The Assumption

THROUGH all the childhood of Christ's Church His Mother was a source of strength and wisdom. She had first shown her Son to Jewish shepherds and held Him up for the adoring Gentile kings. Now she could talk of Him to the infant Church, recalling all the things she had pondered in her heart over the years, through joy, sorrow and glory. Mary knew His mind as no one else could, and we may well believe that the apostles came to her for enlightenment on many facts of His life.

There would be another reason for holding her in special veneration. *She was His Mother,* and her soul was most fit to receive the gifts of the Holy Spirit. We know from the lives of great saints like Teresa of Avila and Francis of Assisi that their interior holiness shone through their physical appearance like light through a window. What must it have been with God's Mother! Her tranquil beauty was informed with a radiance not of this world. Others prayed—her life was a prayer.

The apostles, too, remembered all those occasions during the public ministry of Our Lord when Mary had been their hostess, looking after them with the alert kindness she revealed at the marriage feast of Cana: so quick in wishing to save others from embarrassment, so maternal in her care for the children of men. She had become the Mother of the infant Church with a heart for all who were troubled or in need. It can hardly be doubted that while she lived all those who sought Christ came to look on her holiness and beauty. Wherever she went, the reverent whisper accompanied her, "It is the Mother of the Lord."

From the agony of the cross Jesus had given His beloved disciple John the guardianship of His Mother. Tradition maintains that the Blessed Virgin lived with John to the end of her days. It also asserts that their home was in Jerusalem and that after Mary's assumption, John became bishop of Ephesus.

From the description quoted in the Acts of the Apostles we can learn something of life in the early Church. Unity was the great watchword: unity in worship, the breaking of bread, unity in prayer at all the assemblies of the faithful, unity in daily life like a religious community today, unity in the common treasury and care for the poor and the sick. It was anything but a retired life.

New converts were being made every day, new fields were being opened up all over the Roman empire. There were public baptisms, confirmations, and the laying on of hands for the new priests ordained for the service of the rapidly growing Church. That Our Lady would have been involved in all these events can hardly be doubted, since they were all part of the burgeoning kingdom of her Son.

Of the Assumption itself the Bible makes no mention. It is deduced from certain clear premises. Like Our Lord, the Blessed Virgin was exempt from any stain of original sin. Because of this, she was exempt from the great penalty of original sin—death with its attending corruption. Christ died and because of His own power rose to life in His spiritualized body three days later. Mary died and, through the power of her Son, was assumed in her glorified body into heaven. Devotion to this mystery was widespread in the early Church. The most ancient tradition asserts it; ancient monuments, mosiacs and paintings picture it for the consideration of the faithful.

As far as can be determined, the assumption was a traditional doctrine of the Church from the earliest days, though it did not find precise description in writing and the liturgy until the fifth century, after the debates about the persons and nature of the Trinity had been largely concluded. Then, at the Council of Ephesus (431), the dogma of the Divine Maternity was proclaimed with a tremendous popular demonstration of approval. This opened the way for a wave of Marian devotions, among them the institution by St. Gregory of the Feast of the Assumption.

It is of extreme interest that the Divine Maternity should have been promulgated with great splendor and joy in Ephesus. St. John, Mary's adopted son, had been its first bishop, and it can hardly be doubted that John's devotion to her should have spread and intensified in the diocese he governed. We may in fact think of it as a Marian center, in which devotion to Mary gradually took the place of worship to Diana.

From thinkers, theologians and mystics, from the sixth century on, came a swelling chorus of tributes to the mystery of the assumption in both the Greek and Roman world. The feast became one of the most loved of the liturgical year, for it seemed to touch with grace even the most lukewarm and hardhearted.

The heart of the mystery is a matter that very much concerns us. In the resurrection and the ascension, Christians see the vivid promise to men that on the last day all the faithful shall rise in glory to inhabit the eternal kingdom of Christ. The colors of that far-off morning redden with deeper promise in the assumption of Mary, who, because of her Divine Maternity, was not required to wait for her reward until the end of time. It is not surprising that the faithful of the world should come to love this mystery, so hopeful in its import for all of us.

There remains, of course, the necessity of picturing the assumption to our minds and hearts in meditating the rosary. In the books of the New Testament there are few helps for us, but a splendid picture in the Apocalypse of St. John does give us a vivid cornerstone on which to build:

"And a great sign was seen in heaven: a woman clothed with the sun, the moon under her feet, and upon her head a crown of twelve stars." APOCALYPSE XII, 1.

Out of this hint from the Apocalypse, Murillo has given us several masterpieces of the Blessed Virgin gloriously ascending into heaven. A splendor of light surrounds her and the luminous and innumerable wings of angels, as she is lifted up to her reward. Many artists of genius have loved the same theme, and a careful examination of their works can help us to visualize the assumption. El Greco, in particular, is wonderfully stimulating.

The visual suggestions we find in great art are helpful, but there are also more important and dramatic sources available to us. They are to be found in the apocryphal gospels of St. Melito and the *Arabian Book of the Passing of the Most Blessed Virgin Mary*. Both books probably date back in their written form to the late decades of the fifth century.

We call these apocryphal gospels, not in any derogatory sense, but because they are in essence partly mystical books whose circulation was restricted to the few. Though they do not have the authority of the canonical gospels, they do enshrine certain golden traditions which have proved useful to the liturgy and the spiritual life of the Church.

St. Melito's gospel, which is less wordy than the *Book of the Passing of the Most Blessed Virgin Mary*, provides a detailed description of the assumption which is enormously helpful for our meditation. We first see Our Lady grieving over the absence of her Son. Suddenly a shining angel appears to Mary bearing a great palm branch glittering with celestial light. God's messenger announces that in three days her soul will depart from her body. The palm is from Paradise and it is to be carried before her bier on the way to burial.

Our Lady asks that all the apostles be brought from their missionary labors to be with her at the end. Her wish is granted by the angel.

Mary prepares herself for the end by prayer and meditation. The apostles are carried by the power of God to the house where Mary receives them with joy.

For three days they "sing the praises of God," and the whole Church of Jerusalem joins them in this praise. Suddenly, sleep falls on the multitude; Mary, her virgin handmaids and the apostles are the only ones left there awake.

"Refulgent light falls on the house. It is Our Lord coming with a blazing retinue of angels singing sweet songs of praise.

"Then the Saviour spoke saying: 'Come, thou most precious pearl, enter into the treasury of eternal life.' "

A tender meeting follows between Mother and Son, in which Mary makes known her last requests. They are granted immediately. Our Lord bids His Mother not to fear death, for no harm will come to her, since He will be there to help her and welcome her to paradise. Reassured by these words, our Lady composes herself on her couch and quietly dies.

Following the death of Our Lady, Jesus commands Peter and the apostles to bear the body of His Mother to a new tomb awaiting it in the valley of Josaphat. When the virgin-serving maids prepared to wash the body for burial it could not be looked at because "of the exceeding flashing of light and a great splendor appeared in it . . . and a great sweetness of fragrance issued from it, so that nothing like that sweetness could elsewhere be found." There was also a choir of angels making sweet melody, and a ring of light like the radiance about the moon circled the bier.

The apostles in procession bear the body to the new tomb. They are commanded to wait before the door of the sepulcher for three days. At the end of this time the Saviour appears and speaks with His apostles. The archangel Michael rolls the stone from the sepulcher. Our Lord summons His Mother from the tomb saying, "Rise up My love, and My kinswoman: thou that did not suffer corruption by union of the flesh, shalt not suffer dissolution of the body in the sepulcher.

"And immediately Mary rose up from the grave and blessed the Lord, and fell at the Lord's feet and worshipped Him saying, 'I am not able to render Thee worthy thanks, O Lord, for Thine innumerable benefits which Thou hast vouchsafed to grant unto me Thy handmaid. Let Thy name be blessed for ever, Redeemer of the world, Thou God of Israel.'

"And the Lord kissed her and departed, and delivered her to the angels to bear her into paradise."

Our Lord gave the kiss of peace to the disciples along with a promise to be with them to the end of time.

"Immediately when the Lord had so said He was lifted up in a cloud and received into heaven, and the angels with Him, bearing the blessed Mary into the paradise of God."

It is all here, the music, the radiance, the tenderness of Our Lady's departure from this world, borne up in her light-inwrought body into the paradise of God. It is the vision of her that the heart craves. There is fitness in it, that no defilement of decay should ever touch her virginal purity and that she should not have to wait for her final reward until the general resurrection, when the bodies of all the faithful shall arise from the dead to be with God in His heaven for eternity.

It was this look back into the past and forward into the future that inspired Francis Thompson to write in celebration of the assumption:

Who is She, in candid vesture,
  Rushing up from out the brine,
Treading with resilient gesture
  Air, and with that Cup divine?
She in us and we in her are,
  Beating Godward: all that pine,
Lo, a wonder and a terror—
  The Sun hath blushed the Sea to Wine!

She is indeed bearing us up to God in her tenderness and maternal heart for us. She also bears the first fruits of the resurrection in her lucid and transfigured flesh—like a rainbow of promise to all of us, that we too one day shall rise glorious and immortal in the resurrection of the dead.

O Star of the Sea, daystar of hope, shine down upon us from the glory of your refulgent assumption. Keep us ever in the light of your strength and holiness. Keep us faithful that we may be able to look forward to our own glorified resurrection—now and at the hour of our death.

THE FIFTH

GLORIOUS MYSTERY

The Coronation of Our Lady in Heaven

BEFORE we can picture the fifth glorious mystery we must ask ourselves a question. What is heaven like? In trying to answer the question we shall probably discover that our ideas on the subject are vague, since we can only guess what heaven is like. We are not, however, without some resource for the building of a picture in our minds.

The New Testament offers us considerable help, in the Apocalypse. In this final book of the New Testament, St. John, the beloved disciple, draws a series of vision-pictures of the things to come at the end of the world.

In a swift-moving narrative, we see the final triumph of God over Satan and over the world and its leaders who follow his dark directives. Next comes the general judgment of mankind. All men are to receive justice according to their good and bad deeds. Then, finally, comes the vision of paradise:

"And I beheld a new heaven and a new earth; for the first heaven and the first earth were departed, and the sea is no more. And I saw the holy city, the new Jerusalem, coming down out of heaven from God, prepared as a bride adorned for her husband. And I heard a loud voice from the throne, saying, 'Behold the dwelling of God with men, and He shall dwell with them; they shall be His peoples, and God Himself shall be with them. And He shall wipe away every tear from their eyes, and death shall be no more, neither shall mourning or wailing or pain be any more, because the first things are passed away.'

"And He who sitteth upon the throne said, 'Behold, I make all things new.' And He saith, 'Write: for these words are faithful and true.' And He said to me, 'It is done! I am the Alpha and the Omega, the beginning and the end. To him that thirsteth, I will give of the fountain of the water of life, freely. He that conquereth shall inherit these things; I shall be his God and he shall be My son.' " APOCALYPSE, XXI, 1-7.

All things that we know shall be made new. The city of God will shine like a radiant bride on her wedding day, and the glorified bodies of men will no longer be exposed to evil, sorrow and pain. It is a return to Eden and perfect joy.

Speaking of the new Jerusalem St. John is even more explicit:

"The radiance thereof was like to a stone most precious, to a jasper stone, crystal clear. It had a great and high wall, with twelve gates; at the twelve gates were twelve angels, and names were inscribed thereon, the names of the twelve tribes of Israel. On the east were three gates, and on the north, three gates; and on the south, three gates; and on the west, three gates. And the wall of the city had twelve foundation stones, and on them were the twelve names of the twelve apostles of the Lamb.

"And he that spoke to me had for a measure a golden rod, wherewith to measure the city and its gates and its walls. The city lieth foursquare, and the length thereof is as great as the breadth. He measured the city with his rod, twelve thousand furlongs; the length and breadth and height thereof are equal. He measured also the wall, one hundred and forty-four feet, by man's measure, which is angel's measure.

"And the material of the wall was jasper; and the city was pure gold, like unto pure glass. The foundation-stones of the wall of the city were adorned with every kind of precious stone. The first was a jasper; the second, a lapis lazuli; the third, an agate; the fourth, an emerald; the fifth, a sardonyx; the sixth, a cornelian; the seventh, a chrysolite; the eighth, a beryl; the ninth, a topaz; the tenth, a chrysoprase; the eleventh, a jacinth; the twelfth, an amethyst. The twelve gates were twelve pearls; each gate was formed of a single pearl. And the street of the city was pure gold, transparent as glass.

"I saw no sanctuary therein, for the Lord God almighty is the sanctuary thereof, and the Lamb. And the city hath no need of the sun or of the moon to shine upon it, for the glory of God enlighteneth it, and the lamp thereof is the Lamb. And the nations shall walk by the light thereof, and the kings of the earth bring their glory thereto, and the gates thereof shall never be shut by day—for night shall not be there—and they shall bring thereunto the glory and the honor of the nations. And there shall not enter therein aught unclean, nor that practiseth abomination and falsehood, but only they that are written in the book of life of the Lamb.

"And he showed me the river of the water of life, bright as crystal, issuing forth from the throne of God and of the Lamb, in the midst of the street of the city. On either side of the river was the tree of life, which beareth fruit twelve times, yielding every month its own fruit, and the leaves of the tree are for the healing of the nations.

"And there shall no more be aught accursed. And the throne of God and of the Lamb shall be in the city, and His servants shall minister before Him, and they shall behold His face, and His name shall be on their foreheads, and night shall be no more, and they shall have no need of the light of a lamp or the light of the sun, because the Lord God shall be their light; and they shall reign for ever and ever." APOCALYPSE XXI, 11–27 and APOCALYPSE XXII, 1–5.

Here St. John is giving us the brightest possible lures for the imagination. We need not try to estimate the length and breadth of the holy city from the measurements given in the Apocalypse. They are merely clues to the vast spaciousness of the holy place.

In using the most precise things he can conjure up to describe heaven, such as gold and a catalogue of precious stones, St. John is building up for us a transcendent picture of glittering beauty in which light seems crystallized and from which it is refracted in rays of brilliance and color.

No temple is needed in the City of God. In the midst of the immortal and the pure, there is no longer need for the light of sun or moon, because of the eternal radiance of the Lamb of God.

A shining river is there, and trees bearing fruits. It is a place of happiness, light, peace and contentment, in which man finds the beauties of earth transfigured and transformed like his own glorified body.

From these hints of what heaven will be like, the apocryphal gospels, and especially *The Book of the Passing of the Most Blessed Virgin Mary*, paint a series of childlike and brilliant pictures of Our Lady's entry into heaven.

It is Our Lord Himself who meets Our Lady and shows her the wonders of the demesne over which she is to be the queen. The splendor, we are told, is "more than the eye of man can bear."

At the bidding of her Son, Mary lifts up her eyes. She sees "bright and shining mansions and the glorious crowns of the martyrs." From these blinding sights Our Lady rests her eyes on the "fragrant and lofty trees" from which there breathes a perfume of which "no one can tell." Our Lord plucks fruit from the trees that His Mother may taste how delicious it is, and then leaves her to herself to explore the magnificence of heaven.

Our Lady beholds the wonders of the three heavens with their "treasures of light," and adoring angels. Next she examines the heavenly city, the new Jerusalem. Passing through the various doors, she is praised by the great choirs of angels, the entire host of heaven and all the powers of the universe: lightning, thunder, rain and dew.

At the ninth door Gabriel and Michael with other angels "fell down before her," and at the tenth door, "the sun, the moon and all the planets worshipped her."

The prophets and the just praised Mary at the eleventh door. Then, as the blessed Virgin came through the twelfth portal, "she beheld her Son seated upon a bright throne and encompassed about with a great light. She bowed before the majesty of the Father, the Son, and the Holy Spirit."

Our Lord reveals the secrets of past and present to His Mother, and even shows her the depths of hell, where men suffer for their rebellion and sin.

It is at this point that Mary is seized with sadness. "She besought the Lord to take pity on sinners, begging Him to deal kindly with them, in as much as man is a weak creature. And the Lord gave her His word that He would do so."

In these scenes, described with the innocence and enthusiasm of a child, we can nevertheless see some of the greatest qualities attributed to Mary by saints and scholars. She is indeed the beloved of God, queen of heavenly hosts, and all the powers of the world and the universe, that bow down before her. She is also the great Mother, "seized with sadness" at the lot of sinners. She pleads to her Son for them, and for all men in sorrow and travail. And her pleading is not in vain.

Why did the devotees of Mary in the golden days of the rosary think of the final mystery as the coronation of the Virgin in heaven? The answer is not hard to find. The seventeenth and eighteenth centuries were also the golden age of kings. The crowning of a king and a queen was invested with the most solemn ritual, the most absolute splendor. The golden thrones, the glass carriages, the trappings of purple and scarlet, the ermine and bejewelled crowns—all were part of a solemnity that outranked everything a man might see in his lifetime.

But there was something more implied in the ceremony. The conferring of the crown was a public sign of honor. It was also a proclamation of a queen's right to the unquestioned love and fealty of her people. The queen, in her turn, could be expected to intercede for her loyal subjects, interposing her womanly sense of pity between the justice of the king and those who besought her favor.

Above all the queens of earth, Mary's loving subjects deemed her most worthy to wear the diadem, and that is why they proclaimed her queen of heaven. In her litany they hailed her as queen of angels, queen of patriarchs, queen of prophets, queen of apostles, queen of all saints.

Since no man knows what happened when Our Lady entered heaven, we can only guess about it. Our hearts tell us she is worthy to be a queen. Our minds lead us to speculate on her glory in heaven.

It is obvious that once she assumed glorified flesh and the reward of being God's perfect instrument, Mary's earthly qualities of beauty, purity, modesty, and humility shone forth like morning stars for all to see. She is indeed the tower of ivory, the house of gold, the ark of the covenant and all the other shining titles the poetic hearts of men called her. In heaven her perfection shone forth like a massive and perfect diamond, that all might behold how worthy she was to be the Mother of the Son of God.

She above all others, since she is the mother of Jesus, is able to lead us the easiest way to Him. She best can teach us to love Him as God made man, because she knows Him best, and is quickest and most eager to tell us about His beauty and virtues. She is the mystical rose, because the heart of that rose is aflame with the love of Christ.

It is with justice, then, that our apocryphal gospel returns us to a beautiful picture of Mary's adopted son, St. John, telling us about the shape of things to come in the last days of the world.

St. John shows us that there is judgment implied in Mary's coronation as queen of heaven and the universe. Her perfect correspondence with God's will and grace is a reproach to lukewarmness and sloth. We need her mother's heart. We need our Mother's help.

In the light of that judgment, in the need of that unfailing help, we may well pay homage to her with the words the *Book of the Passing of the Most Blessed Virgin Mary* puts in the mouth of St. John:

"O my Mother, may salvation attend you! May your blessing fall upon all to whom you turn your gaze. I trust in your prayers and in your intercession. Free the world from sorrow, and grant men to walk in paths of truth and justice. May God's love never be wanting to Adam and to the children of Adam; for they are creatures fashioned by the hand of the Lord. May the enemy of mankind be cast out from among them, by the Lord's mercy.

"And the blessed Mary said, 'Amen.'"

BIBLIOGRAPHY

Attwater, Donald and Thurston, Herbert, S.J., (eds.). *Butler's Lives of the Saints, New and Revised Edition.* 2 vols. New York: P. J. Kenedy & Sons, 1949.

Bishop, Jim. *The Day Christ Died.* New York: Harper & Brothers, 1957.

Bussard, Paul. *The Meaning of the Mass.* With a Foreword by Felix M. Kirsch, O.F.M. New York: P. J. Kenedy & Sons, 1942.

Caramen, Philip, S.J. and Dougherty, John J. (eds.). *The Catholic Bible in the St. Peters' Edition.* Portion used for this work was *The New Testament in the Westminster Version of the Sacred Scriptures.* New York: Hawthorn Books, 1958.

Claudel, Paul. *La Rose et le Rosairie.* Paris: Egloff, 1947.

Crawley-Bovey, Mateo, SS.CC. *Rosary Meditations: meditations on the mysteries during the recitation of the rosary as encouraged by Pope Leo XIII.* New York: Benziger Brothers, 1951.

Daniel-Rops, Henri. *The Book of Mary.* Translated from the French by Alastair Guinan. New York: Hawthorn Books, 1960.

De Fleury, Rohault. *La Sainte Vierge.* 2 vols. Paris.

Escriva, José Maria. *Holy Rosary.* Chicago: Scepter, 1958.

Gasquet, F. A., O.S.B. "An English Rosary Book of the Fifteenth Century," *The Downside Review,* (December, 1893).

Gorman, Ralph. *The Last Hours of Jesus.* New York: Sheed & Ward, 1960.

Guardini, Romano. *Le Rosaire de Notre Dame.* Translated from the German by J. Ancelet-Hustache. Paris: Bloud and Gay, 1950.

Heaney, J. M. P. *A Short Treatise on the Rosary.* New York: n.d.

Leather, F. John. *The Rosary: Its Power and Its Use.* London: Sands & Co., 1933.

Louis Marie Grignion De Montford, St. *The Secret of the Rosary.* Translated by Mary Barbour. Bay Shore: Montford Fathers, 1954.

Meschler, Moritz, S.J. *The Garden of Roses of Our Lady: the excellence of the rosary and the best method of reciting it.* New York: Benziger Brothers, 1907.

Morton, H. V. *This is the Holy Land, a pilgrimage in words and pictures.* With an Introduction by Fulton J. Sheen and photographs by Yousuf Karsh. New York: Hawthorn Books, 1961.

Orchard, Bernard, O.S.B.; Sutcliffe, Edmund, S.J.; Fuller, Reginald; and Russell, Ralph, O.S.B. (eds.). *Catholic Commentary on Holy Scripture.* With a Foreword by Bernard Cardinal Griffin. New York: Thomas Nelson & Sons, 1953.

Pace, Edward A., et al. (eds.). *The Catholic Encyclopedia:* New York: Gilmary Society, 1936.

Riciotti, Giuseppe. *The Life of Christ.* Translated from the Italian by Alba I. Zizzamia. Abridged and edited by Aloysius Croft. Milwaukee: Bruce Publishing Company, 1952.

Shaw, James Gerard. *The Story of the Rosary.* Milwaukee: Bruce Publishing Co., 1954.

Sheen, Fulton John. *The Life of Christ.* New York: McGraw-Hill Book Co., 1958.

Thurston, Herbert, S.J. Articles in *The Month,* October, November, December, 1900; January, February, March, April, 1901; August, September, 1902; May, June, 1908; February, 1913; April, June, 1916; and October, 1924.

Willam, Franz Michel. *The Rosary, Its History and Meaning.* Translated from the German by Edwin Kaiser, C.PP.S. New York: Benziger Brothers, 1953.

Ward, Maisie. *The Splendor of the Rosary.* New York: Sheed & Ward, 1945.

An Introduction To The Celebrated Devotion Of The Most Holy Rosary To Which Is Annexed A Method Of Saying It. According To The Form Prescribed By His Holiness Pius V Of The Holy Order Of Preachers. With Some Additional Reflections Upon The Mysteries. London: n.d.

THE AUTHOR AND HIS BOOK

FRANCIS BEAUCHESNE THORNTON, *who was born in Chippewa Falls, Wisconsin, in 1898, studied, in turn, at St. Paul's College in Washington, D.C. (1921–1924), St. Paul's Seminary in Minnesota (1925–1928), Notre Dame University (where he received his A.B., summa cum laude), Columbia University (M.A. in 1933) and Oxford University (B. Litt. in 1937). He entered the Priesthood in 1928. He was professor of English at Duquesne University (1937–1940); associate editor at the* Catholic Digest *(1940–1942); chaplain in the Canadian Army (1942–1946). After World War II he continued working at the* Catholic Digest, *becoming book editor in 1950 and editor of the Catholic Digest Book Club in 1955. He is the author of* On Wings of Song *(Wanderer Press, 1928),* Bitter Wine *(Wanderer Press, 1930),* Return to Tradition *(Bruce, 1948),* How To Improve Your Personality By Reading *(Bruce, 1949),* King Doctor of Ulithi *(Macmillan, 1950),* What's your Catholic I.Q.? *(Kenedy, 1951),* Alexander Pope: Catholic Poet *(Farrar, Straus, 1952),* The Burning Flame *(Benziger, 1952),* Catholic Shrines of the U.S. and Canada *(Funk, Wilfred, 1954),* Cross upon Cross *(Benziger, 1955),* Sea of Glory *(Prentice-Hall, 1953),* The Donkey Who Always Complained *(Kenedy, 1956), and* Catholic Bible for Young People *(Funk, Wilfred, 1958), and many poems and magazine articles. He is also the author of the following titles in the* Shrines Of The World *series (Catholic Digest, Inc.):* St. Peter's In Rome *(1958),* St. John Lateran In Rome *(1958),* Our Lady of Loreto *(1958),* St. Joseph's Oratory in Montreal *(1959),* Our Lady Of The Cape In Canada *(1959),* Our Lady of Martyrs, Auriesville, New York *(1959), and* Jesuit Martyr's Shrine In Canada *(1959). He lives in Port Washington, New York.*

THIS IS THE ROSARY *(Hawthorn, 1961) was designed by Ernst Reichl. The body type is Cloister, a Linotype rendering of Nicolas Jenson's Venetian face of 1470. The type face used for the chapter numbers and titles is Trajanus, a new Venetian type by the American type designer Warren Chappel. Type was set by the Atlantic Linotype Co., Inc., Brooklyn, New York. The book was printed on White Rose Vellum stock, manufactured by the P. H. Glatfelter Co., Spring Grove, Pennsylvania. Printing and binding was by American Book-Stratford Press, Inc., New York City.*

A HAWTHORN BOOK